THE COOKBOOK
FINE AUSTRIAN CUISINE

Alexandra Winkler (Ed.)

Recipes: Werner Pichlmaier
Editorial Assistance: Birgit Schwaner
Translation: Mý Huê McGowran

Photos: Michael Rathmayer

pichler verlag

Sacher. The original. Since 1832.
Over time, run as a family business bound to
tradition and yet still in tune with the times.
With this cookbook we would like to give you
a little piece of Sacher to take home with you.
Our chef, Werner Pichlmaier, continues the
successful history of the Sacher cookbooks, and
has put together for you the trusted, timeless
and traditional Sacher classics, as well as
highlights of Austrian and international cuisine –
modern and light, yet no less tasteful, and newly
interpreted.
Wishing you great enjoyment and success
with your cooking!

Families Gürtler and Winkler welcome your
feedback!

Dkfm. Elisabeth Gürtler   Georg Gürtler B.A.

Mag. Alexandra Winkler   Mag. Matthias Winkler

Speisenfolge

am 27. April 1916.

Kalbskopfsuppe

Seezunge auf Hausfrauenart

Garniertes Rindfleisch

Steirische Hühner

Salat

Kompott

Gansleberpastete

Äpfel mit spanischem Wind

Käse

Obst

Contents

Hotel Sacher Wien

HOTEL SACHER WIEN is one of the most magnificent luxury hotels in the world in one of the most culturally important cities in Europe. Vienna is the cradle of psychoanalysis and a city of musicians, artists, philosophers and architects. Some of our hotel guests have included Indira Gandhi, Queen Elizabeth II and John F. Kennedy. Our history and our first-class location fill us with pride. We offer our guests a unique combination of charming tradition, excellent service and the most modern furnishings and amenities.

Above: *Deluxe Junior Suite Béatrice et Bénédict*

Opposite page, above: *Restaurant Rote Bar* (left) · *Restaurant Anna Sacher* (right)
Opposite page, below: *Blaue Bar* (left) · *Marble Hall* (right)

Hotel Sacher Salzburg

HOTEL SACHER SALZBURG is situated in the culture metropolis of Salzburg, on the banks of the Salzach river. It was formerly an Austrian court hotel and, since 1988, has been part of the Sacher family.

HOTEL SACHER SALZBURG is the epitome of the unique Sacher philosophy: combining the traditional with modern, luxurious comfort. As also in our hotel in Vienna, music plays a big role in HOTEL SACHER SALZBURG. Here, in Mozart's birth city, world famous musicians, international politicians, business people, artists and many other well-known celebrities are our regular guests.

Opposite page, above: *Superior Junior Suite in HOTEL SACHER SALZBURG*
Opposite page, below: *HOTEL SACHER SALZBURG at night*

Above: *Restaurant Zirbelzimmer* (left) · *Sacher Bar* (right)
Below: *Lobby Lounge* (left) · *Winter garden with a breathtaking view of the Salzach river and the Old Town of Salzburg* (right)

Café Sacher

Enjoy in unique locations in the provinces of Austria:
The Sacher Cafés in Vienna, Salzburg, Graz and Innsbruck are the perfect places to get to know traditional Austrian coffeehouse culture. Treat yourself to one of our fine coffee specialties and a piece of the ORIGINAL SACHER-TORTE.

Opposite page: *CAFÉ SACHER WIEN in the 1950s. Photo: Karl Scherb*

Above: *CAFÉ SACHER WIEN* (left) · *CAFÉ SACHER SALZBURG* (right)
Below: *CAFÉ SACHER INNSBRUCK* (left) · *CAFÉ SACHER GRAZ* (right)

Original Sacher-Torte

A Genuine Piece of Vienna

Since 1832, the ORIGINAL SACHER-TORTE has been the most famous cake in the world.
The original recipe remains the well-kept secret of our hotel. Moist, fluffy chocolate cake is refined with apricot jam.
This delicious cake is perfected with a fine chocolate frosting. THE ORIGINAL SACHER-TORTE is entirely hand-made by our experienced confectioners.

Triumphal March around the World

The history of the world-famous ORIGINAL SACHER-TORTE began in 1832, when the almighty "coach-man of Europe," Prince Klemens Wenzel von Metter-nich, ordered that an especially delectable desert be created for his esteemed guests: "Be sure not to bring shame on me tonight!" Precisely for this occasion, the head chef was indisposed and the order was given to the 16-year-old apprentice chef, Franz Sacher. How the lively "bua" [boy] came up with the recipe is still a secret today.

What is clear is that the cake by Franz Sacher tasted exceptionally good to the guests. Throughout his apprenticeship the young chef remembered his stroke of genius. His apprenticeship years took Franz Sacher to the court of Prince von Esterházy, first to Pressburg and then to Budapest. And when the qualified cook took the plunge to becoming self-employed, he offered his successful cake creation to the public once again – this time on a larger scale. And Franz Sacher succeeded with it. The "cake by this man Sacher" was soon in high demand every-where, and the triumphal march around the world of the most famous of all cakes began.

12 Huitres d'ostende 3.80

Wien, *24./10* 189*6*

Frühstück-Speisen.

	fl.	kr.
Oeufs à la Toulousienne	1	40
Omelette au Jambon		70
Tête de veau vinaigrette	1	80
Côte de Porc aux Radis	1	
Escaloppes de veau en casserolle aux pommes	1	35
Rostbraten aux vignons	1	–
Rognons sauté à la viennoise		80
Filets de Sole à la Walewska	2	50

	fl.	kr.
Hors à oeuvres	2	–
Caviar non salé	1	50
Saumon fumé	1	20
Pâté de foie gras	1	–
Pâté de Gibier	1	–
Galantine de volaille		80
Radis au beurre		35
Bouillonhäring		35

Hors d'oeuvres.

			fl.	kr.
1	Dutzend	Whitstable Austern	3	80
1	Portion	Caviar mit Butter	1	50
1	„	geräucherter Lachs	1	20
1	„	geräucherter Lachs mit Caviar	1	50
1	„	Kieler Sprotten	–	35
1	„	Sardellen	–	35
2	Stück	Sardines de Nantes	–	50
1	„	Jäger-Häring naturel	–	35
1/2		Jäger-Häring garnirt	–	45
1		Ostsee-Häring	–	35
1		Bouillon-Häring	–	35
1	Portion	Rettig mit Butter	–	35
1	„	Gansleber-Pastete	1	–
1	„	Wild-Pastete	1	–
1	„	Galantine von Huhn	–	80
1	„	Mayonnaise von Fisch	1	–
1	„	Mayonnaise von Huhn	1	–
1	„	Prager Schinken	–	70
1	„	Westphäler Schinken	–	80
1	„	Zunge	–	70
1	„	Gänsebrust	–	80
1	„	kalter Aufschnitt	1	–
1	„	sauce tartare	–	50
1	„	Trüffel à la serviette	5	–
1	Dutzend	Austern grillirt	4	30
1	Portion	Coquilles von Austern	2	50
1	„	Schinken mit Ei	1	–
1	„	englischer Speck mit Ei	–	90
1	„	gerührte Eier	–	50
1	„	gerührte Eier mit Trüffel	1	20
1	„	gerührte Eier m. geräuch. Lachs	1	–
1	„	gerührte Eier mit Schinken	–	70
1	„	gerührte Eier mit Käse	–	70
1	Omelette mit Caviar		1	20
1	Omelette aux fines herbes		–	70
1	Omelette aux champignons		–	80
1	Omelette mit Nieren		–	80
1	Omelette mit Sardellen		–	70
1	Omelette mit Trüffel		1	20
1	Stück Ei à la coque		–	15
3	„ Eier auf der Platte		–	70
2	„ Eier à la cocote		–	50
3	„ pochirte Eier au jus		–	70

Breakfast, Starters & Soups

Souffléed Egg
with Alba truffles and creamed spinach

INGREDIENTS

4 eggs
4 soufflé dishes
2 tbsp butter for greasing
the dishes
1 small Alba truffle
(truffle slicer!)
Salt

CREAMED SPINACH

200 g (7 oz.) spinach leaves,
cleaned, blanched, well
squeezed and patted dry
20 ml (1 tbsp) reduced, hot
chicken stock
1 tbsp truffle butter
Nutmeg, freshly grated
Salt
Freshly ground pepper

❶ Clean and blanch the spinach leaves and pat them dry. Put in the blender and mix together with the chicken stock. Then strain the spinach mass through a fine sieve and season with salt, pepper and freshly grated nutmeg. Melt the truffle butter and stir in the spinach mass until it has a creamy consistency. Cover and keep warm.

❷ Grease the soufflé dishes with butter. Cover them with aluminum foil so that it hangs over the edges. Now, separate the egg whites from the yolks of the four eggs and make sure that that the individual yolks remain intact and don't burst. (Recommended: prepare four small bowls and let one yolk carefully glide into each one.)

❸ Beat the egg whites with a pinch of salt until stiff and transfer into a pastry bag. Squeeze the egg whites into the soufflé dishes so that the bottom and the sides are covered. Carefully place an egg yolk in the middle of each dish and cover with the rest of the beaten egg whites.

❹ Now cover the dishes with the remaining aluminum foil and place in a warm bain-marie (80°C/175°F). Poach, covered for 6 minutes.

❺ For serving, first put the spinach cream in the middle of the plates. Then carefully remove the souffléed eggs from the dishes and aluminum foil and place on top of the spinach. Finely slice over the truffles.

TIP: Instead of truffles you can also use bacon-bread croutons (for recipe, see p. 21).

Omelet
with spring vegetables

INGREDIENTS

12 eggs
500 g (18 oz.) seasonal vegetables (e.g. carrots, peas, asparagus, wild garlic, spinach leaves)
Chives
1 dollop of cream
80 g (2.8 oz) shortening
Salt, freshly ground pepper

❶ Clean, cube and blanch the vegetables. Whisk the eggs and the cream with an egg whisk; add salt and pepper. Heat up 20 g (0.7 oz) shortening in a frying pan and pour in a quarter of the egg mixture. Stir continuously with a fork, swiveling the frying pan around. Shortly before the eggs thicken, distribute about a quarter of the vegetable cubes over them.

❷ Using a spatula, push the omelet towards the middle of the frying pan and turn it over onto a plate. Repeat this process three times. The omelets should remain slightly creamy inside and golden brown outside. Finally, sprinkle with herbs.

TIP: You can also mix herbs into the cubed vegetables – for example, chives, garden cress, parsley or others, as desired.

Original Sacher-Trüffelschinken-Kipferl
Kipferl with Original Sacher Truffle Ham

Yields approx. 10

INGREDIENTS
1 pkt. pastry
130 g (4.5 oz.) original
  Sacher truffle ham,
  finely diced
1 shallot, finely chopped
Some parsley, chopped
2 egg yolks
2 tbsp crème fraîche
Some cooking oil
Salt
Freshly ground pepper

❶ In cooking oil, sweat the finely cubed shallot and then mix in the finely diced ham, crème fraîche, one egg yolk, parsley, salt and pepper.

❷ Roll out the pastry and cut into triangles of approx. 8 cm (3 inches). Place the filling close to the broad side of the triangle. Now roll the individual pasty triangles in from the bottom towards the triangle point. Bend the ends up for a typical kipferl (croissant) form.

❸ Now whisk the rest of the egg yolk with an egg whisk. Brush the kipferl with the egg yolk, place on a tray covered with baking paper and put in the oven, preheated to approx. 240°C (460°F).

❹ Bake for about 10 minutes until golden brown.
Serve at room temperature.

TIP: You can also serve a chive sauce with the kipferl (for recipe, see p. 54).

Scrambled Eggs
with pumpkin seed oil and bacon-bread croutons

INGREDIENTS
12 eggs
60 g (2 oz.) shortening

BACON-BREAD
CROUTONS
4 slices rye bread, cubed
90 g (3 oz.) bacon, cubed
Genuine pumpkin seed
  oil
Chives
Salt, freshly ground
  pepper

❶ In a bowl, beat and stir the eggs – but not completely – you should still be able to tell the whites from the yolks. Add salt and pepper. Heat shortening in a frying pan, add the eggs and over low heat slowly let them thicken, using a fork to pull them apart in a cross-wise fashion.

❷ At the same time, in a second pan, lightly brown the bacon. Add the bread cubes and fry both until crispy.

❸ Arrange the scrambled eggs on plates; place the bacon-bread croutons on top. Dribble over the pumpkin seed oil and sprinkle with chopped chives.

TIP: For these scrambled eggs, you should use 100-percent "genuine" Styrian pumpkin seed oil. Don't use kernel oil, which is mixed with another vegetable oil.

Breakfast & Starters

Sacher

INGREDIENTS

600 g (1.3 pounds) beef tenderloin
4 shallots, finely chopped and
   blanched
1 bunch parsley, olive oil
Some Tabasco sauce
Salt, freshly ground pepper

SPICE PASTE

4 cornichons
1/2 tbsp salted capers
4 anchovy filets
3 tbsp ketchup, 1 tbsp Dijon
   mustard

MUSTARD MAYONNAISE

Mayonnaise (amount as for recipe
   on page 55)
3 tbsp coarse Dijon mustard
Salt
Freshly ground pepper

FOCACCIAS

25 g (1 oz) yeast, 250 g (2 cups)
   flour
30 ml (2 tbsp) olive oil
Rosemary, chopped
5 g (1 tsp) salt

❶ For the focaccia, dissolve the yeast and salt in 175 ml (6 fl. oz.) of lukewarm water and, with the flour, knead into a tough dough. Drizzle the olive oil over the dough and let rise for 20 minutes at room temperature. Then form the dough and oil into a flatbread of approx. 2 cm (1 inch), place on a tray covered with baking paper and again let rise for 20 minutes. Preheat oven to 220°C (425°F), sprinkle the focaccia with rosemary and bake approx. 20 minutes until golden brown. Allow to cool.

❷ For the spice paste, mix all the ingredients into a fine paste in a food processor.

❸ For the mustard mayonnaise, stir together the mayonnaise and Dijon mustard, add salt and pepper.

❹ Now finely chop the cleaned and well-cooled meat and place in a bowl. Add shallots, parsley and spice paste. Mix everything well, season to taste and finish with a dash of olive oil. Cut open the focaccia and fill with the beef tartar. Spread with mayonnaise and garnish with herbs.

TIP: Tuna tartar can also be made using this recipe. Instead of using beef tenderloin, simply use tuna. Instead of mayonnaise, avocado cream goes nicely.

Sacherstangerl · Bread Rolls
with tuna spread

Yields 20 rolls

INGREDIENTS

20 oblong-shaped rolls, as desired
125 g (1/2 cup) canned tuna
2 hard-cooked eggs, chopped
1 onion, chopped and blanched
60 g (2 oz.) pickles, chopped
1/2 tbsp capers, chopped
75 g (3 oz.) QimiQ
125 g (1/2 cup) quark
1/2 tbsp Dijon mustard
Some Tabasco sauce
Salt
Freshly ground pepper

● Mix all the ingredients together to form a creamy mass. Make lengthway incisions into the rolls and pull them apart slightly to allow an opening for the cream. Fill the mass into a pastry bag with a smooth nozzle and squeeze into the opening. Garnish as desired – for example, with half a quail egg.

Sacherstangerl · Bread Rolls
with radish spread

Yields 20 rolls

INGREDIENTS

20 oblong-shaped rolls, as desired
**240 g (1/2 pound – 1 small bunch)
  radishes**
25 g chives
125 g (1/2 cup) QimiQ
125 g (1/2 cup) quark
**125 g (1/2 cup) Gervais (brand of
  Austrian cream cheese)**
Some Tabasco sauce
Salt
Freshly ground pepper

● Grate the well-washed radishes, salt, let draw briefly and then pat them dry. Finely cut the chives. Combine the QimiQ, Gervais and quark and stir until creamy; mix well with radishes and chives. Make lengthway incisions into the rolls and pull them apart slightly to allow an opening for the cream.

Fill the radish mass into a pastry bag with a smooth nozzle and squeeze into the opening. Garnish as desired – for example, with chives or cheese cubes.

Sacher Tafelspitzsulz · Tafelspitz Aspic
with cornsalad

INGREDIENTS

600 g (1.3 pounds) cooked Tafelspitz (boiled beef)
600 ml (2.5 cups) beef stock
2 carrots
2 turnips
1/4 bulb of celery root
4 tbsp chives, chopped
10 leaves gelatin, soaked in cold water
Salt, freshly ground pepper
Some oil for the tray

CORNSALAD SALAD

200 g (7 oz.) cornsalad (also known as lamb's lettuce)
4 tbsp corn oil
2 tbsp beef stock
3 tbsp apple vinegar
Salt

❶ First, add 200 ml (1 cup) of water to the stock and then boil. Peel carrots, turnip and celery root. Then, using a peeler, cut them into thin strips (diameter approx. 3 mm/0.1 inch), add to the stock and cook until soft. Remove the vegetable strips from the soup and let cool.

❷ Pat dry the gelatin soaked in cold water and dissolve it in the soup. Add salt and pepper to the soup and remove from the stove. Grease a terrine mould with oil and place aluminum foil on top length ways. (The aluminum foil should cover the terrine as smoothly as possible. If needed, you can use some kitchen paper to smooth it down.)

❸ Now cut the Tafelspitz into thin slices using a bread-cutting machine (diameter approx. 2 mm/0.08 inches). Dip each slice in the still warm soup and then line the mould with it. Make sure that that slices of meat hang over the mould by about 6 cm/2.3 inches (later they will be folded inwards).

❹ Pour some soup into the terrine mould, sprinkle with 1/3 of the chopped chives. Lengthways, place over about 1/3 of the vegetable strips. Repeat this process – dipping the Tafelspitz slices in the soup, placing in the mould, sprinkling over chives; vegetables – another three times. Finally, pour the rest of the soup into the mould and fold in the overlapping pieces of meat. Cover well with the aluminum foil and refrigerate for about 3 hours.

❺ For the cornsalad salad, shortly before serving the dish, whisk the corn oil, the beef stock and vinegar with an egg whisk. Add salt to taste and marinate the salad with it. Then turn the terrine upside down on a plate and remove the aluminum foil. Cut the aspic into slices. Arrange it, together with the salad, on cooled plates.

TIP: You can also sprinkle over some finely chopped chives. Pumpkin seed pesto also tastes good with the dish.

Butterhead Salad

with bread and crispy goat's cheese

INGREDIENTS

- 1 butterhead salad (especially tender butter, head or romaine salad)
- Fresh herbs (cress, chives or chervil)
- 4 pieces Picandou (goat's cheese)
- Approx. 4 slices toast without crust
- 2 black nuts*, cut in slices
- 4 tbsp shortening

DRESSING

- 5 tbsp walnut oil
- 2 tbsp white balsamic vinegar
- 2 tbsp vegetable stock
- Some sugar
- Pepper, freshly ground
- Salt

❶ For the dressing, mix the oil, vinegar and stock together well; add salt and pepper to taste. Remove the outer leaves of the salad, and use only the inner, crispy leaves. Save a few herbs for the garnish, finely plucking apart the others. Clean and wash the salad and herbs well and dry in a salad spinner.

❷ Cut out round shapes from the toast, about as small as the cheese. Place one piece of cheese between 2 slices of bread and press together. Cut the rest of the toast in strips of about 1 cm/0.4 inch. Fry in the butter until golden brown, then let them drain on kitchen paper. Keep warm.

❸ Now mix the salad and herbs with the dressing and distribute it on a plate. Decoratively arrange the cheese, crispy bread strips and the sliced black nuts on top: garnish with herbs.

TIP: *"Black nuts" are walnuts that are pickled while still green. You can find them in delicatessens. Otherwise, you can replace them with roasted walnut kernels.

Marinated Asparagus
with Bryndza-cheese dumplings

INGREDIENTS

20 nice stalks of white asparagus, same thickness
100 g (3.5 oz.) sugar/snow peas, cut in diagonal strips
1 yellow turnip, finely diced
5 tbsp melted butter
1 stale bread roll
Juice from 1 lemon
1 pinch of sugar
Salt
Freshly ground pepper

VINAIGRETTE

5 tbsp asparagus stock
2 tbsp white balsamic vinegar
3 tbsp grape seed oil
4 tbsp olive oil
Some lemon juice
Salt
Freshly ground pepper

BRYNDZA-CHEESE DUMPLINGS

200 g (7 oz.) bryndza cheese (alternatively, sheep's or goat's cheese)
3 tbsp heavy cream, whipped
Juice from 1/2 lemon
1 tbsp olive oil
White pepper, freshly ground
Salt

TRIMMINGS

4 quail eggs, boiled, possibly pickled
Edible blossoms
Chervil

❶ Peel the asparagus and cut off the woody ends. Then, in boiling salted water, cook al dente along with the stale bread roll, lemon juice and a pinch of sugar. Drain and keep aside about 5 tbsp of the asparagus stock for the vinaigrette. Put the asparagus in an oven-proof dish, dribble over the melted butter and cover with aluminum foil. Keep warm in an oven preheated at 80°C (175°F).

❷ For the vinaigrette, mix the lukewarm asparagus stock with white balsamic vinegar, grape seed and olive oil and season to taste with salt, pepper and lemon juice. Pour into an elongated dish, add the warm asparagus and allow to cool and steep in the vinaigrette.

❸ Bring a small pot of water to the boil, add salt and blanch the finely diced turnip and peas until al dente. Douse with ice water and drain in a sieve.

❹ For the dumplings, season the cheese with lemon juice, salt and pepper to taste. Fold in the whipped cream, stir in the olive oil, until it forms a creamy mass. Refrigerate for 15–20 minutes.

❺ To serve, put five pieces of asparagus on each plate with a little vinaigrette. Place the turnip and peas in the vinaigrette, let it soak in; add salt and pepper and pour some over the asparagus. Then, form the cheese dumplings using two spoons – re-dipping them in hot water, otherwise the cheese will stick. Place 2 dumplings per plate on top of the asparagus.

TIP: The asparagus will be finer and more delicate in taste the longer it stays in the vinaigrette. It can therefore be prepared a few hours' in advance.

BY THE WAY: Bryndza cheese is a special type of sheep's cheese from Slovakia and the Polish Carpathians. It is originally thought to have originated from Transylvania, but has been manufactured in Slovakia at least since the 14th century. Today it carries the EU registration "Protected Designation of Origin (PDO)." In Austrian cuisine, bryndza is the main ingredient for Liptauer that includes paprika powder. Alongside Grammelschmaltz, Liptauer is served in every heuriger (wine tavern) as a spread.

Breakfast & Starters

Marinated Beef Filet

with asparagus, morels and curly endive salad

INGREDIENTS

400 g (14 oz.) beef filet
30 g (1 oz.) garden herbs
    (parsley, chives, chervil,
    basil)
8 stalks asparagus
200 g (7 oz.) fresh small
    morels
Handful of endive leaves
1 stale bread roll
Juice from 1 lemon
Olive oil
Salt, freshly ground pepper

MARINADE

2 tbsp walnut oil
1 dash white balsamic
    vinegar

❶ Prepare the filet one day ahead. Chop the herbs and mix together on a plate. Season the beef with salt and pepper; rub with olive oil and coat with the chopped herbs. Put the meat in aluminum foil, roll it up tightly and then, additionally, roll it in aluminum foil. Put in the freezer and freeze briefly. (After freezing, the meat should still be able to be cut, that means, if you're using a bread-cutting machine, the meat can be a little harder and left to freeze longer.)

❷ The next day, peel the asparagus and remove the woody ends. In a pot of salted water, cook the stale bread, lemon juice and a pinch of sugar; add the asparagus and cook al dente. Douse with ice water.

❸ Clean the morels, rinsing with cold water; dry. Briefly sauté in olive oil. Let cool. Clean the endive, rinsing with cold water; dry with a salad spinner.

❹ For the marinade, mix together some walnut oil and white balsamic vinegar; add salt and pepper. Cut the asparagus into bite-size pieces. Marinate the asparagus, morels and salad.

❺ Take the beef out of the freezer, unpack it and cut into very thin slices. Arrange the pieces on four plates; sprinkle with some salt and pepper; dribble with olive oil. On top, nicely place the marinated asparagus, morels and the salad.

TIP: What makes all the difference to the taste here is mainly the quality of the beef filet.

Original Sacher Goose-Liver Torte

based on a recipe by Hans Peter Fink

For a 22 cm (8 inches) Ø cake base (12 pieces)

INGREDIENTS

1 Sacher-Torte cake base, approx. 5 mm/0.2 inches high, Ø 22 cm/8 inches (see page 119)
200 g (7 oz.) goose liver terrine
100 g (3.5 oz.) bitter dark chocolate, at least 70% cocoa
2 cl (4 tsp) old apple brandy or Calvados

GOOSE LIVER MOUSSE

350 g (12 oz.) goose liver terrine (see p. 48)
200 ml (1 cup) cream, whipped half stiff
4 leaves gelatin, soaked in cold water
2 cl (4 tsp) port
Salt

APRICOT FILLING

100 g (3.5 oz.) dried apricots
1 tbsp Périgord truffle cubes (available in delicatessens)
1 tbsp white balsamic-apple vinegar
1 tbsp sugar

ICE WINE GLAZE

2 leaves gelatin, soaked in cold water
50 ml (3 tbsp) consommé or strong beef stock
50 ml (3 tbsp) ice wine

❶ For the mousse, heat up the port and dissolve the already soaked and drained gelatin at approx. 60°C (140°F). Mix some cooled port and gelatin mixture into the room-temperature goose liver terrine. Then strain through a fine sieve; salt. Carefully fold in the not-too-cold, half-whipped cream.

❷ For the apricot filling, finely cube the dried apricots. Bring a pot filled with 250 ml (1 cup) water to the boil; add the apricot cubes, sugar and vinegar and simmer for 10 minutes. Add the truffle cubes and let cool.

❸ Place aluminum foil on a flat tray. Melt the couverture in a warm bain-marie. Spread it as thinly as possible – and to about the diameter of the cake base – over the aluminum foil. Place the base over the couverture and put on the cake hoop. Then dribble with apple brandy or Calvados and brush the cake base with approx. 1 cm (0.4 inches) of the goose liver mousse. Cut the terrine in slices of about 5-6 mm (very, very thinly), and place these – more in the center, about 1.5 cm (0.6 inches) away from the edge – on the mousse layer. Put another layer of mousse on the slices – this time about 5 mm – and spread over the prepared apricot filling, also more in the center. Put some more mousse on top, spread smoothly and refrigerate the torte for an hour.

❹ Meanwhile, prepare the ice wine glaze. Heat up some beef stock and dissolve the 2 soaked, squeezed out gelatin leaves in it. Pour in the rest of the soup and add the ice wine; stir everything together.

❺ Remove the torte from the fridge, cover with the glaze and place in the fridge again for an hour. Then carefully remove the cake ring; divide the torte into pieces.

❻ Serve together with some apricot chutney or preserved cranberries. And, if you want to garnish the torte with preserved rowan berries, you will increase the taste sensation of this special, savory-sweet variation of a Sacher-Torte even more with a new, interesting nuance.

TIP: In Hotel Sacher, hazelnut brioches are served with this dish. Simply prepare a brioche pastry and sprinkle with hazelnut flakes before you put it in the oven.

Breakfast & Starters

Classic Viennese Beef Soup

INGREDIENTS

300 g (10.5 oz.) beef for boiling
300 g (10.5 oz.) bones from beef
350 g (12.3 oz.) herbs and vegetables for making soup (without carrots)
1 small bunch lovage
2 onions with skin
1 leek
1 bay leaf
A few peppercorns
Salt
Freshly ground pepper

❶ Wash the meat and bones under running cold water; dry with kitchen paper. Cut the meat into cubes and, together with the bones, place into cold water and blanch briefly. Then douse with cold water and put back in the pot. Cover with water and slowly bring to the boil, constantly skimming off the froth. Now add the herbs and, simmering gently, cook for about 2–2 1/2 hours. Halve the onions leaving the skin on; with the cut surface facing down, brown in a heated frying pan (without oil). Then – about an hour prior to the end of the cooking process – to the pot with the meat and bones, add the onions, along with the washed herbs and vegetables, leek and lovage.

❷ Finally, strain through a straining cloth, and season with salt to taste.

❸ Before serving, as desired, add one of the Viennese soup garnishes described on the following pages. Sprinkle with chives or parsley.

Semolina Dumplings

INGREDIENTS

100 g (3.5 oz.) coarse semolina
1 medium-sized egg (50 g/1.7 oz.)
40 g (1.4 oz) butter, room temperature
Nutmeg, grated
White pepper, freshly ground
Salt

❶ Place the room temperature butter in a bowl and beat until fluffy. Add the egg and mix with the butter. Stir in the semolina. Season with salt, pepper and nutmeg and let sit for 10 minutes.

❷ Bring some water to the boil in a large pot and add salt. Using two spoons, dipping them into warm water to clean, form dumplings from the mass and place in the boiling water. Allow to boil once; douse with cold water and, covered, let sit for about 20 minutes.

TIP: A tasty variation on these dumplings are truffle-semolina dumplings. To make them, simply work some finely sliced, preserved black truffles into the dumpling batter.

Frittaten · Crêpe Slivers

INGREDIENTS

2 eggs
100 ml (7 tbsp) milk
60 g (2 oz.) flour, fine
Shortening (for frying)
Salt

❶ Whisk the 2 eggs with the cold milk. Together with the salt and flour, mix well into a thin crêpe batter. Heat the butter in a flat frying pan (crêpe frying pan). Pour in enough batter to thinly cover the base of the pan – if need be, distribute the batter by swirling the pan around. First fry one side of the crêpe until golden brown, then turn it over and brown the other side. Remove from the pan and continue the same process with the rest of the crêpes (add more butter if necessary) until all the batter is used up.

❷ Let the crêpes cool, then roll up each crêpe and slice finely with a sharp knife.

❸ Before serving, distribute the cut pancakes into four soup bowls. Pour in the hot beef soup and sprinkle with finely chopped chives or parsley.

TIP: Instead of butter, you can also use oil to fry the crêpes – they're a bit lighter this way but don't lose anything in taste.

In addition, working some finely cut chives or parsley into the batter will give you herb-flavored crêpes.

Veal Liver Dumplings

INGREDIENTS

160 g (6 oz.) veal liver
2 pieces of chicken liver
1 shallot
1 clove garlic
1–2 tbsp parsley, chopped
Marjoram

1 slice of toast, without crust
40 g (1.4 oz) breadcrumbs
1 egg
Milk (for soaking)
3 tbsp lard or oil
Salt
Freshly ground pepper

❶ Finely chop the shallot. Heat up the lard or oil in a frying pan and sweat the shallot. Allow to cool.

❷ Soak the toast in slightly warmed milk. Wash the veal and chicken liver, pat them dry, clean and then, together with the shallot and the well-drained toast, grind finely in a meat grinder. Finely chop the garlic clove, parsley and fresh marjoram.

❸ In a bowl, combine the liver-toast mass with the egg, bread-crumbs, garlic, parsley and marjoram and season with salt and pepper. Cover and refrigerate for about 20 minutes.

❹ Bring a large pot of water to the boil and add salt. Using wet hands, form dumplings from the mass (or mould the dumplings using 2 spoons) and then put them in simmering salted water for about 8 to 10 minutes.

TIP: You can also fry the liver dumplings in oil, instead of boiling them. This more hearty variation is particularly appreciated in Vienna.

Cream of Asparagus Soup
with radishes and chicken oysters*

INGREDIENTS

600 g (1.3 pounds) Marchfeld asparagus
3 shallots, peeled and diced
1 l (4.2 cups) chicken stock
200 ml (0.8 cup) cream, 200 g (7 oz.)
crème frâiche
80 g (3 oz) butter, a pinch of sugar
Salt, freshly ground pepper

GARNISH

16 chicken oysters (alternatively,
chicken liver or breast)
1 tbsp chicken juice, 1 sprig of thyme
Butter for frying

GARNISH

3 radishes, finely cut
Chervil leaves

❶ Peel the asparagus. Cut off the tips for the garnish and blanch. Cut the rest of the asparagus stalks into small pieces. Peel and cube the shallots.

❷ In a pot, heat up and melt the butter, briefly sweat the shallots. Add the asparagus stalks and likewise briefly sweat. Pour in the chicken stock and simmer everything for about 15 minutes. Then mix in the cream and crème fraîche and let simmer for another 5 minutes. Afterward, finely purée the asparagus soup with a hand blender and pass through a sieve. Season with salt, pepper and a pinch of sugar.

❸ For the chicken oysters, melt the butter in a frying pan and sear the chicken pieces. Add the previously blanched asparagus tips and briefly toss. Season with salt, pepper and thyme.

❹ Froth up the asparagus soup with a hand mixer. Place the chicken oysters and asparagus tips in deep plates and pour over the soup. Garnish with finely cut radishes and chervil leaves.
(*Chicken oysters are the two small, round pieces of dark meat on the back of chicken near the thigh.)   **Photo, right**

Frothy Spinach Soup

INGREDIENTS FOR SOUP BASE

3 tbsp butter
200 g (7 oz.) potatoes, peeled and cubed
100 g (3.5 oz.) celery root, peeled and
cubed
50 g (1.7 oz.) leek, only the white part
100 g (3.5 oz.) onions
1.5 l (6.5 cups) chicken stock
250 ml (1 cup) heavy cream
50 g (1.7 oz.) crème fraîche
Nutmeg, freshly grated
Salt, freshly ground pepper

SPINACH PASTE

500 g (18 oz.) spinach leaves, blanched
and blended

❶ For the spinach paste, blanch the spinach leaves, let drain and blend.

❷ For the stock, foam the butter in a pot. Add the onion, leek, celery root and the potatoes and briefly sauté everything. Add the stock, season and let simmer for about 30 minutes. Afterward, stir the heavy cream and crème fraîche into the soup and bring to the boil again. Then, using a hand blender, finely purée the soup and strain through a sieve; season again. Add the spinach paste and blend it all together with the hand blender.
Photo, page 70

Viennese Potato Soup

Yields 4 to 6 portions

INGREDIENTS

1.5 liters (6.5 cups) beef stock (see page 34)
300 g (10.5 oz.) potatoes
100 g (3.5 oz.) fresh mushrooms, mixed (chanterelles, king oyster mushrooms, porcini, etc.)
120 g (4 oz.) root vegetables (carrots, celery root, yellow turnip)
50 g (1.5 oz.) onions
1–2 garlic cloves, crushed
50 g (1.5 oz.) bacon
1 dash of dry white wine
125 ml (1/2 cup) heavy cream
1 tbsp flour
4 tbsp shortening
1 bay leaf
Some marjoram
Caraway, ground
Salt
Freshly ground pepper

GARNISH
Chives, finely cut

❶ First, peel and chop the onions; peel the potatoes and root vegetables, then cut the potatoes into about 1 cm (0.4 inch) cubes. Chop carrots, celery root and turnip into small cubes. Clean the mushrooms (with a damp cloth) and cut the caps off. Slice the mushroom stalks into bite-size pieces.

❷ Heat the butter in a casserole and sweat the chopped onions. Add 1/3 of the cubed potatoes, 1/3 of the cubed vegetables and all the mushroom stalks. Fry for some minutes, dust with flour, deglaze with white wine. Pour in 1.25 l (5.2 cups) of beef stock (keep 250ml/1 cup). Bring to the boil. Add bay leaf, marjoram, garlic and caraway, salt and pepper. After the soup has cooked for around 10 minutes, remove the bay leaf, purée the soup with a hand blender and pass through a sieve.

❸ Put the remaining 250 ml (1 cup) beef stock with the rest of the potatoes and vegetables in a pot, place on the stove and heat up. Cook the cubed vegetables for about 10 to 15 minutes until soft.

❹ Meanwhile, finely dice the bacon and fry in a pan. Add the mushroom caps and fry in the bacon.

❺ Then add the fried mushroom caps and the steamed vegetables as well as the potato cubes to the soup. Mix in the cream. Bring the soup to the boil again; add salt and pepper. Serve in prewarmed soup bowls and with sprinkled chives.

BY THE WAY: The potato soup is justifiably considered a real classic of Viennese cuisine. But what today is frequently forgotten is that the soup traditionally gets its typical taste from the highly aromatic Neusiedl marjoram (a special type of marjoram from the Pannonian realm). However, this marjoram was almost unavailable for many years and was considered almost extinct until individual farmers in northern Burgenland were found to still have plants. Today the Neusiedl marjoram is being farmed again (www.neusiedler-majoran.at) and gladdens the palates and hearts of all lovers of Viennese taste.

Foamed Parsnip Soup
with crawfish

INGREDIENTS
600 g (1.3 pounds) parsnips
3 shallots, peeled and cubed
1 liter (4.2 cups) chicken stock
500 ml (2 cups) heavy cream
60 g (2 oz.) butter
Salt
Freshly ground pepper

IN ADDITION
16 crawfish

❶ Place the crawfish together with some caraway seeds and dill in boiling salted water and simmer for 2 minutes. Douse with ice water. Detach the tails from the bodies; break off the claws. Press the tails together a little until the shell cracks and breaks. Remove the flesh (also the intestinal threads) and refrigerate.

❷ Wash and peel the parsnips. Cut one into fine cubes for the garnish and blanch. Cut the rest into slices. Melt the butter in a pot and sweat the shallots. Add the parsnip slices; salt and braise briefly. Pour in the chicken stock, bring to the boil and simmer for about 15 minutes. Then mix in the cream and let simmer for a further 5 minutes. Afterward, finely purée with a hand blender, pass through a sieve and season with salt and pepper.

❸ Melt a small piece of butter in a frying pan, add the blanched parsnip slices and sauté. Add the crawfish and toss briefly.

❹ Before serving, warm up the soup and foam up with a hand blender. Place the parsnip slices and crawfish in the middle of the soup bowls and pour over the foamed soup.

Frothy Pumpkin Soup

with butter schnitzel and pastry salt sticks

INGREDIENTS

500 g (18 oz.) pumpkin, peeled and cubed
1 yellow bell pepper, cored and diced
2 shallots, peeled and diced
1 clove garlic, finely cut
1 liter (4.2 cups) chicken stock
500 ml (2 cups) cream
30 g (1 oz.) butter
1 pinch of caraway seed powder
Salt
Freshly ground pepper

BUTTER SCHNITZEL

300 g (10.5 oz.) veal, finely minced
2 egg yolks
2 bread rolls, soaked in milk and strained
1 tsp white breadcrumbs
Shortening (for frying)
Grated lemon zest, untreated
Nutmeg, freshly grated
Salt, freshly ground pepper

SALT STICKS

Pastry dough
1 egg yolk
Caraway seeds, whole
Sea salt, coarse

❶ If desired you can also make the pastry bread sticks a few hours earlier. To make them, roll out the pasty and brush with the egg yolk; sprinkle with caraway seeds and sea salt. Put in the freezer briefly to freeze it. Then cut the pastry into strips with a knife and place them on a tray lined with baking paper, put into a preheated oven. Bake at about 180°C (350°F) for approx. 10 minutes.

❷ For the soup, heat up the butter in a pot and sweat the diced shallots. Add the pumpkin and bell pepper cubes and the garlic; mix well and add salt and pepper. Let braise briefly; pour in the chicken stock, bring to the boil and simmer for about 15 minutes. Then mix in the cream and simmer for a further 5 minutes. Purée in a blender (or using a hand blender) and strain through a sieve. Season with caraway powder, salt and pepper.

❸ For the butter schnitzel, take all the ingredients – minced veal, egg yolks, breadcrumbs, breadcrumbs, and the soaked bread rolls – and mix together. Season with grated lemon rind, salt and pepper and refrigerate. Then, form small patties from the meat mass using your hands. Heat the butter lard in a frying pan and sear the patties on both sides. Afterward, at 160°C (320°F) in a preheated oven, finish cooking for about 10 minutes.

❹ Place the butter schnitzel in the middle of the plate, pour over the soup, place a salt stick on the plate.

TIP: The soup can be rounded off with toasted pumpkin seeds and few drops of pumpkin seed oil.

Dîner du 8 Septembre 1886.

Potage à la Poméranienne.

Filets d'esturgeon à la vénitienne.

Pièce et côte de boeuf.

Salmis de perdreaux à la Rachel.

Dindons rôtis, salade, compote.

Pouding de cabinet.

Fromages.

Glaces aux framboises et au caramel.

Dessert.

Side Dishes & In-Between Dishes

Strudel Pastry

INGREDIENTS

1/4 kg (1 cup) plain flour
Flour for the tea towel etc.
Approx. 1/8 liter (1/2 cup) lukewarm water
1 tbsp vegetable oil
Vegetable oil for brushing
A pinch of salt

❶ Because strudel pastry has to sit for a long time, it's best to prepare it a half day or a full day in advance. To do this – ideally using a food processor – combine the flour, lukewarm water, vegetable oil and salt and knead. Let sit for 10 minutes. Then knead into a smooth, elastic dough. Form into a ball, brush with oil and refrigerate for at least 4 hours, or overnight. After this time, sprinkle some flour on a tea towel and roll out the dough on it (make the corners more round than square). Dust your hands with flour and pull the dough out thinly. Here's the best way to do it: first, use the back of your hands to carefully spread the edges of the pastry outwards. Then, with flour-dusted hands, put your hands under the center of the dough. Turn your hands over and then, using the backs of your hands – continually moving them back and forth – pull and stretch the dough outward until the strudel pastry is evenly thin all around and almost seems transparent.

❷ Brush the finished pastry with melted butter and fill 2/3 of it with a savory or sweet filling. Then, using the tea towel, roll it together and fold up the edges. Carefully place it on a greased tray (or one with baking paper). You can also brush it with a beaten egg yolk, and put it into a preheated oven. Baking time and temperature will vary depending on the filling.

Quark Shortcrust Pastry
For an onion tart, savory tarts, etc.

INGREDIENTS

100 g (3.5 oz.) quark, 20 % fat
1 egg
300 g (10.5 oz.) flour, smooth
200 g (7 oz.) butter, in small pieces
2 pinches of salt

● Prepare the shortcrust pastry quickly (it doesn't tolerate much heat and ought to be done quickly and placed in the fridge immediately). First, combine the butter, cut into small pieces, with the flour, quark, the egg and salt and knead it into a dough. Then wrap the pastry in aluminum foil and let it sit in the fridge for about 2 to 3 hours – or longer. Shortcrust pastry dough will keep in the fridge for a few days (but use as an ingredient the freshest possible, long-lasting quark), so you can prepare it well in advance. The measurements given here are for a tart or spring form pan with a diameter of 28 cm (11 inches).

TIP: To make a shortcrust pastry to use as a base for a sweet tart or fruit pie, replace the quark in this recipe with the same amount of superfine sugar, also use less salt and, additionally, some vanilla pulp (from a vanilla bean) and grated lemon zest (of 1/2 an untreated lemon) and work it into the dough.

Erdäpfelschmarren
(Type of oven-baked hash browns)

INGREDIENTS

300 g (10.5 oz.) potatoes
3 egg yolks
3 egg whites
2 tbsp crème fraîche
2 tbsp shortening
Salt
Freshly ground pepper

● Bring a pot of water to the boil and boil the potatoes until soft; peel while still warm. Pass the potatoes through a potato ricer and combine well with the crème fraîche and the 3 egg yolks. Whisk the 3 egg whites together with a little salt until stiff. Now fold the potato mass carefully into the egg whites; add salt and pepper. Heat up the shortening in a non-stick pan; pour in the mixture and put in a pre-heated oven for about 10 minutes at 190°C (375°F). Pull apart the finished schmarren with a fork, arrange on prewarmed plates.

Fried Potatoes

INGREDIENTS

600 g (1.3 pounds) potatoes
1 onion
1 sprig rosemary
Shortening or oil for frying
Some caraway seeds, whole
Salt

● Peel the raw potatoes, cut into appropriate pieces and boil them in a pot of salted water with some caraway seeds for approx. 15 minutes (depending on size, a bit longer). Peel and quarter the onion and sauté in small frying pan with some shortening or oil. In a larger pan, heat up the butter or oil (or a mixture of both). Add the cooked, well-drained potatoes to the pan as well as the onion and the rosemary sprig. Fry the potatoes golden brown and season with salt. Before serving, remove the rosemary and also the onion pieces, if desired.

Potato Purée

INGREDIENTS

1 kg (2.2 pounds) potatoes
200 ml (0.8 cup) milk
100 ml (0.4 cups) heavy cream
60 g (2.1 oz.) butter
60 g (2.1 oz.) brown butter
  (see: Tip)
Nutmeg, freshly grated
Salt

● Peel the potatoes and boil in salted water until soft. Let steam briefly and then pass through a potato ricer. Heat up the milk and cream in a small pot. Combine with the potato mixture; add the cold and brown butter and stir everything into a creamy purée. Season with salt and nutmeg.

TIP: You can make brown butter yourself – due to its nutty aroma, it's also called nut butter. Heat up at least 250 g (1/2 pound) butter and brown over medium heat while continually stirring (!). Stir until no more foam is formed. Then pass the liquid butter through a sieve lined with a coffee filter or tea towel. Immediately place in a bain-marie filled with ice water and keep stirring – which makes the butter creamy – or refrigerate immediately.

Side Dishes & In-Between Dishes

Sacher

Bread Dumplings

Yields about 6 dumplings

INGREDIENTS

200 g (7 oz.) bread for making dumplings (bread cubes)
2 shallots
2 tbsp parsley, finely cut
3 eggs
100 ml (0.4 cups) coarse flour
Flour for dusting
1 tbsp cornstarch (Maizena)
180 ml (6 fl. oz.) hot milk
50 g (1.7 oz.) butter
Nutmeg, freshly grated
Salt

❶ First, peel the shallots and cut them into small cubes. Heat the butter, add the shallots and sauté until golden brown. Add the chopped bread and mix with the shallots. Toss briefly and then put in a large bowl. In a small bowl, beat the eggs and then combine them with the bread mixture. Heat up the milk; pour it into the bread mixture, then fold into the dough mass. Add the cornstarch, flour, salt, pepper and finally the parsley (if desired, also some more dumpling bread). Knead everything together well. Then let sit for about 15 minutes.

❷ Boil enough salted water in a pot and then reduce the heat. Using damp hands, form round dumplings from the dough, coat with flour, then form again. Finally, place the bread dumplings in simmering salted water and let steep for 15 minutes; every now and then, "shake" the pot a little and make sure that the dumplings rise to the surface. Lift out the dumplings, strain and prepare.

TIP: From the leftover bread dumplings (or napkin dumplings) you can make dumplings with egg. Sweat a finely cut onion in oil or shortening. Cut the dumplings into slices, add to the pan and fry until golden. Beat one egg per person and pour over the onions; allow to thicken; add salt and pepper; sprinkle with finely chopped parsley– and you're done!

Dumplings or Spaetzle

INGREDIENTS

250 g (2 cups) fine flour
2 eggs
1 egg yolk
150 ml (5 fl. oz.) milk
1 tbsp melted butter
Oil for frying
Nutmeg, freshly grated
Salt

● Put eggs, egg yolk and milk in a bowl and stir. Fold in the flour and melted butter; add salt and nutmeg. Using a cooking spoon, stir until you have a smooth batter (add some milk or flour if necessary). Boil some salted water in a large pot. Pass the batter through a dumpling sieve (or a spaetzle grater) and into boiling salted water and cook briefly until the dumplings rise to the surface, then drain. Douse with cold water, let drain. If desired, toss in hot butter or oil.

Bohemian Potato Dumplings

INGREDIENTS

1 kg (2.2 pounds) floury
  potatoes
1 shallot
1 tbsp parsley, finely cut
2 egg yolks
1 white bread roll
40 g (1.4 oz.)
  breadcrumbs
2 tbsp potato starch
Approx. 30 g (1 oz.)
  butter for the
  dumpling filling
100 g (3.5 oz.) butter for
  the crumbs
Nutmeg, freshly grated
Salt

❶ Wash and dry the potatoes. Boil half of them – 1/2 kilo of potatoes – until soft. Place the boiled potatoes on a tray lined with baking paper; bake in a preheated oven at 150°C (300°F). Afterward, peel the potatoes and pass through a potato ricer. Peel the remaining 1/2 kilo of potatoes raw and grate them, add salt, squeeze them out and place in a bowl. Add the boiled, riced potatoes as well as the egg yolks, starch, salt and nutmeg. Mix everything together and knead until you have a smooth batter.

❷ Now prepare the dumpling filling. Finely cube the peeled shallots. Cut the bread roll into small cubes (approx. 5 mm/0.2 inch). Heat up 30 g (1 oz.) butter in a frying pan, sweat the shallot; add the bread cubes together with a tablespoon of finely chopped parsley; add salt and nutmeg. Mix everything together and sauté, seasoning if desired.

❸ Boil some salted water in a large pot. Take a piece of potato dough, flatten it and place on the palm of your hand; put some filling in the middle, then form it into a fine, round dumpling.

❹ Finally, put the potato dumplings in the boiling water and simmer for about 10 minutes. In the meantime, heat up 100 g (3.5 oz.) butter in a pan and fry the breadcrumbs golden brown. Take the finished dumplings out of the water and drain well. Serve sprinkled with butter-crumbs.

Round Semolina Dumplings

Yields 12 small dumplings

INGREDIENTS

100 g (3.5 oz.) wheat
  semolina
1 shallot
1 egg
1 egg yolk
250 ml (1 cup) milk
2 tbsp butter
Nutmeg, freshly grated
Salt

❶ Finely cube the shallot. Heat up the butter in a pot; sauté the shallot until it's glassy. Stir in the wheat semolina, sauté. Pour in the milk and keep stirring; add the salt and nutmeg and continue stirring until the mass loosens from the bottom of the pot. Then remove from the stove, and leave to cool down. Mix the egg and yolk well into the cooled dough mass and refrigerate for 20 minutes.

❷ Afterward, boil some salted water. With wet hands, form small dumplings from the mass and cook for 10 minutes on moderate heat in simmering salted water until they are done.

TIP: You can also find semolina dumplings on page 96 as a side dish to the duck dish. By the way, these dumplings are also tasty with a filling – for example, made from duck entrails, for which you can cook duck liver, heart or stomach, then mince, mix and season.

Sacher

Green Beans with Dill

INGREDIENTS
600–700 g (1-1.5 pounds)
  green beans
200 ml (0.8 cup) hot beef stock
1 tbsp dill tips, finely cut
1 tbsp flour
200 ml (0.8 cup) milk
1 tbsp butter
1 dash of light vinegar or
  apple vinegar
Salt
Freshly ground pepper

● Wash and clean the beans (remove the string) and cut into manageable pieces. In a pot of salted water, cook the beans until tender and then drain. Heat up the beef stock. In a pot, melt the butter; mix in the tablespoon of flour using an egg whisk and pour over the hot stock. Stir using the egg whisk (don't let any lumps form) and heat it up until everything thickens. Reduce the heat and stir in the milk. Add the beans. Mix well and season with vinegar, salt and pepper. Mix in the finely cut dill and then bring to the boil again briefly.

Cabbage, Old-Viennese Style

INGREDIENTS
1 cabbage, weighing about
  1 kg (2.2 pounds)
1 clove garlic
100 g (3.5 oz.) streaky bacon
250 ml (1 cup) hot beef stock
1 tbsp flour
1 tbsp butter
Salt
Freshly ground pepper

● Remove the outer leaves and the cabbage stalk. Cut or finely slice the cabbage. Boil some salted water, add the cabbage and cook through. Strain and let drain. Cut the bacon in very fine, small cubes or grind in a meat grinder. Heat up the butter in a pot; add the bacon and fry. Stir in the flour, cook briefly then pour in the hot stock. Simmer and, meanwhile, constantly stir with an egg whisk – until the liquid has thickened slightly. Then add the cabbage – drained of as much of the water as possible. Mix everything well; season with the finely chopped garlic, salt and pepper and, finally, bring to the boil one last time.

Warm Cabbage Salad

INGREDIENTS

1 head of white cabbage
200 ml (0.8 cup) beef stock
100 g (3.5 oz.) smoked bacon
1 onion
50 ml (1.7 fl. oz.) vinegar
1 tsp caraway seeds, whole
White pepper, freshly ground
Salt

❶ Remove the outer leaves of the cabbage. Quarter it and chop or slice very finely. In a pot, bring the beef stock to the boil with the vinegar, caraway seeds, salt and pepper. Add the cabbage to the stock and, covered, allow to boil vigorously. In the meantime, cube the onions and heat up a frying pan, render the bacon, fry until crispy and remove from the pan. Now add the finely chopped onion to the pan and fry until glassy in the remaining fat.

❷ Remove the cooked cabbage from the stove; pour off the remaining liquid. Put the cabbage in a bowl and combine it with the onions. Distribute the fried bacon cubes over the top. Finally, dribble the remaining fat from the pan over the top.

Creamed Spinach

INGREDIENTS

1 kg (2.2 pounds) spinach
  leaves
1 small onion
1 clove garlic
250 ml (1 cup) hot beef stock
2 tbsp flour
2 tbsp heavy cream
2 tbsp butter
Some nutmeg, freshly grated
Salt
Freshly ground pepper

⬤ Thoroughly wash the spinach and cut off the stalks. Then, either blanch or scald in boiling salted water; drain and strain and purée using a hand blender. Heat up the beef stock. Peel and finely cube the onion and in a pot, sweat in the butter. Stir in the flour and immediately fill with the hot soup. Bring to the boil, continuously stirring with an egg whisk (don't allow any clumps to form). Add the puréed spinach leaves and mix in well. Over low heat, cook for about 10 minutes until the spinach is creamy. Stir in the salt, nutmeg, pepper, finely chopped garlic as well as the 2 tablespoons of cream. Bring to the boil once more. As desired, before serving, place a few flakes of butter on the creamed spinach.

Potato Salad

Yields 4–6 portions

INGREDIENTS

1 kg (2.2 pounds) salad potatoes (kipfler)
500 ml (2 cups) warm beef stock
1 large red onion
1 tbsp Estragon mustard
5 tbsp vinegar
60 ml (4 tbsp) oil
Salt
Freshly ground pepper

GARNISH

1–2 tbsp chives, finely cut

❶ Boil the washed and peeled potatoes in a pot of salted water until soft. Drain the water and let the potatoes sit briefly. Cut them into fine slices while they are still warm and put in a bowl. Heat up the beef stock and pour it over the potato slices; add the vinegar, oil, mustard, salt and pepper and mix everything through well. Then let draw for 30 minutes.

❷ Afterward, finely cut the red onion and mix it in; season again. Garnish with some chives.

TIP: The potato salad is made warm so that it becomes particularly creamy. Should you not have any beef stock or not want to use any, you can also prepare this salad with 1/2 liter (2 cups) of water. Then, only mix the oil with the warm potato slices in the bowl. Boil some water with vinegar, mustard and a pinch of sugar; let cool, pour over the potatoes, season with salt and pepper, mix through, and continue the steps described above.

Potato & Cornsalad Salad

Yields 6–8 portions

INGREDIENTS

1 kg (2.2 pounds) potato salad (see previous recipe)
150 g (5.2 oz.) cornsalad (also known as field salad)
1 clove garlic, pressed
2 tbsp apple vinegar
3 tbsp pumpkin seed oil
Salt

● Wash the lettuce well and dry using a salad dryer. Mix together the pumpkin seed oil, apple vinegar and salt to make a marinade. Put the cornsalad in a bowl and marinate. Then take the prepared potato salad out of the fridge and place in another bowl – rubbed with the garlic. Fold in the cornsalad.

Cucumber-Cream Salad

INGREDIENTS
800 g (1.8 pounds) cucumbers
1 tsp dill tips, chopped
1 clove garlic
200 g (7 oz.) crème fraîche
4 tbsp apple vinegar
White pepper, freshly ground
Salt

● Peel and halve the cucumbers, remove the seeds; slice finely. Then, salt well and leave for approx. 20 minutes. Afterward, squeeze the liquid out of the cucumbers and pour off the water. Stir the apple vinegar with the crushed clove of garlic, pepper and dill (if desired, also add a pinch of confectioners' sugar), and mix well with the cucumber. Combine everything with the crème fraîche.

TIP: The chefs of Hotel Sacher always prepare salads like this using crème fraîche because it has a thicker consistency than sour cream and doesn't become watery as quickly (an advantage for cold buffets).

Green Bean Salad

INGREDIENTS
750 g (1.7 pounds) green beans
1 onion, small
Some vegetable stock (alternatively water)
3 tbsp apple vinegar
6 tbsp vegetable oil
Salt, freshly ground pepper

GARNISH
Some parsley or savory

❶ Clean the beans (remove the string), cut into appropriate pieces and cook in salted water until soft. Then, drain off and douse with cold water; let drain. Peel the small onion peel and cube finely.

❷ Put the beans in a bowl, add vegetable oil and combine well. Add the vinegar, salt, pepper, onion cubes and some vegetable stock (or water) and mix well. Leave for at least 1 hour, stirring every now and then. Before serving, sprinkle with fresh, finely chopped parsley (or savory).

Cold Cabbage Salad

INGREDIENTS
1 head of white cabbage
4 tbsp vinegar
6 tbsp oil
1 tsp caraway seeds, whole
White pepper, freshly ground
Salt

● Remove the outer leaves of the cabbage; quarter it and either cut very finely or use a slicer to slice it. Put the cabbage in a bowl, salt well and let stand for 30 to 45 minutes. Then, drain off the water that has been drawn out by the salt. Squeeze out the extra water from the cabbage. Mix the vinegar, oil and caraway seeds into a marinade and stir into the cabbage. Add pepper, and then mix again well.

Apple Horseradish

INGREDIENTS
3–4 sour apples
30 g (1 oz.) horseradish,
   freshly grated (or from a jar)
1 dash of beef stock
Vinegar
Salt

● Cut up the apples; remove the core and peel. Then, in vinegar water, cook them until soft, drain and purée using a food mill (purée sieve). Season with vinegar and salt; mix well with the horseradish.

TIP: Here's a quick version for preparing apple horseradish: cleave the raw apples, grate finely with a grater, quickly add 2 tablespoons of lemon juice and mix well; stir in with the horseradish, mix and add salt. You can also make the apple horseradish spicier by using a bigger portion of horseradish, round it off with a bit of beef stock or make it a little smoother by adding some oil.

Chive Sauce

INGREDIENTS
3 tbsp finely cut chives
2 slices white bread, without
   crust
2 raw egg yolks
3 hard-cooked egg yolks
1 tsp Dijon mustard, pinch
   of sugar
Milk for soaking
200 ml (0.8 cup) heavy cream
250 ml (1 cup) vegetable oil
1 dash of vinegar
White pepper, freshly ground
Salt

● Soak the bread without crust in the milk. Put the boiled egg yolk through a sieve and mix with the raw egg yolk. Remove the bread from the milk, discard the excess liquid, then purée and mix it with the egg yolk. Add salt and pepper, then, very, very slowly stir the vegetable oil into the mass. It should be thick and smooth, like a mayonnaise. Then add the vinegar, mustard and sugar and stir in the runny cream until the sauce is nicely creamy. Before serving, mix with the fresh, finely cut chives.

Old-Viennese-Style Tomato Sauce

INGREDIENTS

1/2 kg (18 oz.) tomatoes
1 small carrot
1 small onion
1 small bunch parsley
1 thick piece of bacon or
  prosciutto
100 ml (6 tbsp.) white wine
400 ml (13.5 fl. oz) hot beef
  (or vegetable) stock
2 tbsp flour
2 tbsp butter
1 pinch sugar
Some "rosen" paprika powder

● Finely cut the onion. Roughly cut the peeled carrot and tomatoes into pieces. Heat the butter and sweat the onion. Add the carrot, piece of bacon and the bunch of parsley and fry together briefly. Deglaze with white wine; add the tomato pieces and mix everything well and, over medium heat, simmer until the liquid from the tomatoes has totally evaporated. Meanwhile, heat up the stock. Then add some flour to the tomato mixture (to thicken), pour in the hot stock and stir well. Remove the bacon and parsley and strain the sauce through a sieve. Decant into a clean pot and bring to the boil again. Season with the paprika powder and sugar.

Mayonnaise

INGREDIENTS

2 egg yolks
A pinch of mustard
1 dash of Worcestershire
  sauce
1 dash of pickle vinegar
250 ml (1 cup) vegetable oil
Salt, freshly ground pepper

● Place the not-too-cold egg yolks in a bowl. Add mustard, salt and pepper and, using a hand blender, whisk until foamy. Now slowly dribble in the vegetable oil and meanwhile, continue to mix with the hand blender until the mayonnaise has the right, creamy consistency. Season with the pickle vinegar and Worcestershire sauce.

Sacher

Salonbeuschel
(Old-Viennese Salon Offal)

INGREDIENTS

600 g (1.3 pounds) calves' lights (lungs)
1 calf heart
1 calf tongue
1 bunch herbs and vegetables for making soup
6 peppercorns
3 pimento corns
1 bay leaf
1 sprig thyme
1 small onion
40 g (1.4 oz) shortening
30 g (1 oz) flour
Vinegar
Mustard
A pinch of sugar
Marjoram, dried
2 tbsp sour cream
2 tbsp heavy cream
Goulash juice (if on hand)
Some lemon juice
Salt, freshly ground pepper

"BEUSCHELKRÄUTEL"

1 small onion
1 anchovy
1 clove garlic
1 tbsp parsley
1 grated lemon zest

❶ First, clean the lungs and remove the trachea and esophagus. Then soak the lungs well (like a sponge, they should soak up the water right to the core!). Now place the lungs together with the calf heart and tongue in a large pot filled with cold water and bring to the boil. Halve the onion and brown in a hot pan with the cut surface facing downwards.

❷ Then place the browned onion halves, herbs and vegetables for making soup, peppercorns, pimento, bay leaf, thyme and salt with the meat and cook until soft. After about 1 hour, take out the lung and place in cold water to cool down. Cook the heart and tongue for another 30 minutes until they are soft.

❸ Meanwhile, prepare the "Beuschelkräutel" [offal herbs]. Finely chop the onion, anchovy, garlic and parsley and mix with the grated lemon zest.

❹ Remove the heart and tongue from the pot and, likewise, cool in water. Drain the offal stock, then reheat it and cook until it's reduced. Now, cut the lungs, heart and tongue into thin, short strips, removing any cartilage, if necessary.

❺ Heat the shortening in a casserole, sprinkle in the flour and, stirring, fry until brown. Add the offal herbs, stir everything well and let draw over low heat for a few minutes. Now pour in the reduced stock and stir well with an egg whisk; let cook for approx. 15–20 minutes until the sauce has a thick consistency. Now add the offal and tongue strips; season with salt and pepper, vinegar, marjoram, mustard and sugar. Stir in the sour cream and heavy cream and simmer for another 5–10 minutes. Season with lemon juice and place in deep bowls. If available, dribble a tablespoon of hot goulash juice over the offal or place in the middle of the dish.

RECOMMENDED SIDE DISH: bread dumplings (see p. 48).

TIP: Using the additional "salon" in this dish's name implies that the recipe is the more noble variation of the "mean" offal. The ragout, popular in Vienna, made with calves' lungs and heart, originally a dish from the poorer kitchens, is refined here by adding goulash juice and sour cream and made, so to speak, "acceptable for the salon." Should you not have any goulash juice on hand, don't worry! It still tastes good!

Side Dishes & In-Between Dishes

Sacher

Potato Goulash

INGREDIENTS

750 g (1.7 pounds) floury
   potatoes
3 onions
2 garlic cloves, crushed
1 Braunschweiger [smoked
   sausage/sandwich meat]
Approx. 400 ml (13.5 fl. oz)
   hot beef/vegetable stock
1 dash of vinegar
If needed, cornstarch or
   flour for binding
2–3 tbsp shortening or oil
A pinch of marjoram, dried
2 tsp paprika powder, sweet
Some caraway seeds, whole
Salt, freshly ground pepper

❶ Peel the potatoes and cut into sufficiently sized cubes. Peel the onions and cut into small cubes. Heat the shortening or oil in a pot, and, slowly (over low heat) sweat the onions. Remove briefly from the stove. Add paprika powder; pour in the vinegar and stir. Top up with the hot beef or vegetable stock.

❷ Now add the potatoes – the stock ought to just cover them. Stir in the marjoram, caraway seeds and crushed garlic. Then simmer until the juice thickens and the potatoes are cooked.

❸ Now cut the Braunschweiger sausage into slices, add to the soup and let everything simmer for a few more minutes. Should the sauce be too watery, add some cornstarch (Maizena) or flour, then season with salt and pepper.

TIP: Like every goulash, this one also tastes especially good when it has time to sit after it's been cooked (this can be up to a whole day) to be enjoyed later, heated up.

Blunzengröstl

(Fried black sausage and potatoes)

INGREDIENTS

500 g (18 oz.) blunzen (black
   sausage)
500 g (18 oz.) potatoes, waxy
100 g (3.5 oz.) onions
80 g (2.8 oz) pork schmaltz
Some marjoram, dried
Salt, freshly ground pepper

IN ADDITION

1/2 bunch chives
Freshly grated horseradish

❶ Cook the potatoes, then peel and cut into slices. Slice the peeled onions. Pull the skin off the black sausage and then cut it into slices. Now heat the schmaltz in a frying pan and sweat the onions; add the potato slices and fry. Finally, add the black sausage slices and mix everything together; season with salt, pepper and marjoram. Using a roasting jack, press the potato mass together (like making hash browns) and fry crispy on both sides.

❷ Sprinkle the Blunzengröstel with chives and, ideally, serve whole, dividing into portions at the table, with freshly grated horseradish.

TIP: To turn over the Blunzengröstl mass in the pan without breaking it, use a round platter of sufficient size, placing it on top of the pan and holding with a flat hand (don't forget to use pot holders!). Then lift the pan along with the platter so that the unfried part of the gröstl lands face-down on the platter. Then, carefully let it slide back into the pan. **Photo, right**

Szegediner Goulash

INGREDIENTS

600 g (1.3 pounds) pork shoulder
(without rind/fat)
1/2 kg (1.1 pounds) sauerkraut
150 g (5.2 oz.) onions
2 garlic cloves, peeled
1 tsp tomato paste
1/2 tbsp flour
Beef stock or water
100 ml (3.4 fl. oz.) heavy cream
100 ml (3.4 fl. oz.) sour cream
60 g (2.1 oz.) pork schmaltz or oil
1 tsp "rosen" paprika (hot paprika powder)
1 cooking spoon of paprika powder, sweet
2 bay leaves
About 1 tsp caraway seeds, whole
Salt, freshly ground pepper

❶ Clean the pork and cut into bite-size cubes. Peel and chop the onions. Finely chop the garlic. Heat the pork schmaltz or oil (or a mixture of both) in a pot; sweat the onions until golden brown. Quickly stir in both paprika powders. Pour in a little stock or water; add salt, pepper and stir in the meat cubes. Add the chopped garlic, bay leaves and caraway seeds and stew the meat over medium heat for about 1 1/2 hours. After about half of this cooking time, stir in the sauerkraut. If necessary, add water or stock (the liquid should just cover the meat and sauerkraut).

❷ As soon as the meat and sauerkraut are tender, combine the cream, sour cream and flour and stir it into the goulash. Cook for another 10 minutes.

CLASSIC SIDE DISH: bread dumplings or salted potatoes.

Wiener Saftgulasch · Viennese Goulash

Yields 4 to 5 portions

INGREDIENTS

1 kg (2.2 pounds) beef foreshank
900 g (1.9 pounds) onions
1–2 tbsp tomato paste
Dash of vinegar
100 g (3.5 oz.) pork schmaltz or 100 ml
(3.4 fl. oz.) oil
1–2 tbsp tomato paste
3–4 tbsp paprika, sweet
2 garlic cloves, crushed
1 tsp marjoram, dried
1 tsp caraway, chopped or crushed using
pestle and mortar
2 juniper berries, 2 bay leaves
Salt
Freshly ground pepper
Approx. 1.6 liters (7 cups) water

❶ Peel and cube the onions. Clean the beef and cut into cubes of approx. 40–50g (1.4-1.5 oz). Heat the schmaltz or oil in a pot, add the onions and, stirring, fry golden brown. Then add the pressed juniper berries, bay leaves, marjoram, caraway, salt and pepper; fry briefly. Add the paprika and immediately the tomato paste and garlic. Quickly deglaze with about 800 ml (3 cups) water and a dash of vinegar, bring to the boil and add the cubed meat. Cook for at least 2 1/2 hours over low heat until tender (duration depends on the meat quality), stirring from time to time. If necessary, add a little water. When the meat is almost done and the sauce has a creamy consistency, stir well and top up with enough water to totally cover the meat. Now turn up the heat and let the goulash cook through again.

❷ A classic side dish for a breakfast, morning tea, midnight or any-time goulash is the Vienna Kaisersemmel (white bread roll). When serving the goulash as a main or in-between meal, salted potatoes or bread dumplings are recommended.

TIPS: If you want to cook a little "lighter" but not do without the good taste that the schmaltz gives the goulash, only use half the schmaltz and replace the rest with oil. And, a goulash is especially good when you cook a lot of it and give it some more time. It tastes best the next day, when it's rested for a while and is reheated.

Stuffed Peppers

INGREDIENTS

8 green bell peppers
400 g (2 cups) mixed minced meat (half beef / pork)
200 g (7 oz.) cooked rice
2 onions
1–2 garlic cloves, crushed
1 tbsp parsley, finely chopped
Butter for frying / oiling
Marjoram, dried
Salt, freshly ground pepper

TOMATO SAUCE

1 kg (2.2 pounds) ripe tomatoes
2 onions
Juice from 1 lemon
1/2 liter (2 cups) beef stock
2 tbsp tomato paste
Flour for dusting
Butter for sweating
Some sugar
2 bay leaves
Approx. 8 peppercorns
Salt, freshly ground pepper

❶ First, prepare the tomato sauce. Cut the peeled onions into small cubes and sweat them in the butter; stir in the tomato purée. Quarter the washed tomatoes and add; mix everything well and dust with flour. Pour in the beef stock; add the bay leaves, peppercorns, some lemon juice, a pinch of sugar (more, if desired) and the salt and pepper. Boil the sauce and then simmer over medium heat for about 20 minutes. Finally, remove the peppercorns and bay leaves and season again. Purée with a hand blender and strain through a sieve.

❷ Wash and dry the peppers and cut off the tops. Remove the seeds and white flesh with a knife. Also clean the tops. Wash the peppers inside, and dry using kitchen paper.

❸ For the pepper stuffing, peel the onions, cut them finely into cubes and fry in a frying pan with the hot oil until golden brown. Finely chop the parsley, add it and stir in with the onions. Put minced meat in a bowl; mix it with the onion-parsley mixture as well as the egg, crushed garlic, salt, pepper and marjoram. Finally, work in the cooked rice and approx. 1/8 liters (1/2 cup) of water.

❹ Now take the meat-rice mixture and fill the peppers with it. In a suitable pot, heat up the tomato sauce. Place the stuffed peppers in the sauce and then steam over medium heat for approx. 45 minutes; stirring the sauce from time to time.

RECOMMENDED SIDE DISH: salted potatoes.

Grammelknödel

(Dumplings with Crackling)

INGREDIENTS

500 g (18 oz.) floury potatoes
2 egg yolks
100 g (3.5 oz.) coarse flour
Flour for the work surface
2 tbsp soft butter
Butter for frying

FILLING

200 g (7 oz.) crackling
1 bunch parsley, finely
 chopped
1 onion
1 clove garlic, peeled
Butter for frying
1 pinch marjoram, dried
Salt, freshly ground pepper

❶ For the dumpling dough, peel the potatoes and cook until soft. Let stand for a while, then pass them through a potato ricer. Allow to cool.

❷ In the meantime, prepare the filling. Cut the onion finely, heat some butter in a frying pan and fry golden brown. Finely chop the garlic. Pluck the parsley and chop finely. Chop up the crackling. In a bowl, combine the parsley and crackling with the onion, garlic and marjoram. Season with salt and pepper and refrigerate.

❸ Spread the cooled potato mass on a floured surface and knead it, together with the egg yolks, soft butter and flour into one smooth dough (adding flour, if necessary). Pack the dough in aluminum foil and refrigerate for about 15 minutes.

❹ Afterward, form the dough into a roll and cut into 8 slices. Place some filling on each slice using a spoon, mould the dough around the filling to make a nice, round ball. Boil a pot of salted water and put the dumplings in (reduce heat, if necessary). Let the dumplings draw for about 7 minutes in the simmering water, then remove.

❺ Recommended side dish: warm cabbage salad (see p. 51).

TIP: If desired, you can also serve the crackling dumplings with gravy.

Sacher

Baked Ham Pasta

INGREDIENTS

200 g (7 oz.) dried (or home-made) diced & sliced pasta
250 g (1/2 pound) cooked ham
2 eggs, 3 egg yolks, 3 egg whites
150 ml (5 fl. oz.) heavy cream
250 ml (1 cup) sour cream
Butter for greasing
Some nutmeg, freshly grated
Salt
Freshly ground pepper

FOR SPRINKLING

Breadcrumbs

❶ Cook the dried or home-made pasta in a sufficient amount of salted water al dente (no softer, as they will still be baked). Strain and drain well.

❷ Cut the ham into small cubes. Stir in the 2 eggs, 3 yolks, both creams and a pinch of salt. Fold in the ham cubes. Whisk the 3 egg whites with some salt until stiff. Fold the whites into the ham-butter mixture and combine everything carefully with the cooked and cooled pasta. Season with nutmeg, salt and pepper. Then put into a greased, ovenproof dish. Sprinkle over the breadcrumbs, as desired. Distribute a few flakes of butter on top and put in a preheated oven. Bake at 180°C (350°F) for about 45 minutes until the surface is nicely crispy. Arrange on prewarmed plates and serve with lettuce or cornsalad salad.

Onion Quiche "Sacher Eck"

**For a spring or tart form
of 28 cm (11 inches) Ø**

INGREDIENTS

**1 quark shortcrust pastry
500 g (18 oz.) white onions
1 bunch spring onions
1/2 leek
Approx. 150 g (5.2 oz.) lean
   bacon
5 eggs
80 g (2.8 oz) gouda or other
   mild cheese, grated
250 ml (1 cup) heavy cream
8 tbsp olive oil
Butter for greasing
Nutmeg, freshly grated
Salt
Freshly ground pepper**

❶ Prepare the shortcrust pastry according to the recipe on page 46 at least 4 hours ahead and refrigerate.

❷ Peel, halve and slice the onions. Heat the olive oil in a frying pan, and sweat the onions, constantly stirring. Remove from the stove; allow to cool.

❸ In the meantime, grease the form. Put the prepared pastry on a floured surface and roll out thin. Line the spring form with the pastry and evenly distribute the onions over it.

❹ Slice the half leek and the spring onions (only the white bulb) and cut the bacon into small cubes. Grate the cheese. Beat the 5 eggs in a bowl, add the heavy cream and beat with an egg whisk. Combine the leek, spring onions, bacon and grated cheese and season with the nutmeg, salt and pepper. Then pour the mixture over the onions. Put the onion quiche in a preheated oven. Bake at 200°C (400°F) for about 40 minutes. Afterward, let the oven-fresh onion quiche stand for about 10 minutes, then cut and serve.

TIP: If you blind-bake the pastry, it absorbs less liquid (from the onions and egg mass) and is thus drier and crispier at the end. To do this, prick the pastry several times with a fork, place baking paper over the top and fill it with dried peas or beans. Then put it in a preheated oven and bake for 8 minutes at 200°C (400°F); remove the peas and paper and, as described above, continue with the onion mix.

Sacher

ZUR

ERINNERUNG

AN DEN

5. MAI

1900.

Herr

Victor Strzygowski.

Vegetarian Cuisine

Crispy Vegetable Rolls
with radish-sprout salad

INGREDIENTS

Spring roll pastry for 8 rolls
  (2 per person)
1 kg (2.2 pounds) desired
  seasonal vegetables
  (carrots, celery root,
  broccoli etc.)
1 tbsp parsley, chopped
2 eggs
125 g (1/2 cup) sour cream
Egg whites for brushing
Oil for frying
Salt
Freshly ground pepper

RADISH-SPROUT SALAD

1 bunch radishes
1 pkg. sprout mix
1 tbsp cilantro, chopped
4 tbsp peanut oil
2 tbsp white balsamic
  vinegar
1 tbsp soy sauce
Salt
Freshly ground pepper

IN ADDITION

Cilantro sprigs (garnish)

❶ For the filling, wash and clean the vegetables and cut into small cubes. Blanch and douse in ice water. Then combine the cubed vegetables with the chopped parsley, whisked eggs and sour cream. Season with salt and pepper.

❷ Prepare the pastry according to the instructions (if frozen, allow enough time to defrost). Brush each piece with egg white and place the prepared filling on top. Then fold in the ends and roll together tightly.

❸ Heat some oil for frying in a pot.

❹ Meanwhile, wash, clean and cut the radishes into ultra-thin slices (using a vegetable slicer). Wash the sprouts and pat them dry. Stir the peanut oil, white balsamic, soy sauce and chopped cilantro into a marinade; season with salt and pepper and use to marinate the radishes and sprouts.

❺ Fry the vegetable rolls in hot oil until crispy. Drain on kitchen paper. Distribute the radishes on plates and top with sprouts. Place the vegetable rolls on top and garnish with the cilantro sprigs.

TIP: Serve the vegetable rolls with a dipping sauce made from one tablespoon each of paprika paste, mayonnaise and sour cream, mixed together and seasoned.

Spinach Crêpes

with cream cheese and leek

INGREDIENTS

250 g (1/2 pound) potatoes
2 tbsp creamed spinach
4 eggs
125 ml (1/2 cup) milk
130 g (1 cup) flour
Shortening
Salt

FILLING

500 g (18 oz.) spinach leaves,
    cleaned and washed
1 beef tomato
2 shallots
1 clove garlic
250 g (1 cup) cream cheese,
    coarse-grained
2 tbsp parmesan, freshly grated
2 tbsp white breadcrumbs
100 g (3.5 oz.) butter
Butter flakes
Nutmeg, freshly grated
Salt
Freshly ground pepper

IN ADDITION

Frothy spinach soup (see p. 38)
1 bunch spring onions, blanched

❶ For the crêpes, cook the potatoes, peel and let stand briefly, then grate finely. In a bowl, stir the flour with the 4 eggs and the milk into a smooth batter. Add the grated potatoes and the creamed spinach. Mix well; season with salt and let stand for 10 minutes. If not already prepared, you can now cook the spinach soup and spinach paste.

❷ For the filling, blanch the cleaned, washed spinach leaves in salted water; douse in ice water. Strain in a sieve and pat dry, then chop roughly. Blanch the beef tomatoes and remove the skin, core them and cut into small cubes. Peel and finely chop the shallots and the garlic. Now, melt some butter in a frying pan, add the shallots and sweat them. Stir in the garlic, tomato cubes and the chopped spinach; season and pour into a sieve. Allow to cool.

❸ Heat the butter in a pan. Use a small ladle to spoon in the batter, and fry thin crêpes. When the crêpes are finished, combine the cooled spinach with the cream cheese in a bowl. Place a small amount of the spinach-cheese mass on a crêpe and fold into a triangle. Sprinkle some freshly grated parmesan and breadcrumbs over the crêpes and add the butter flakes. Place on a greased baking tray and bake for about 5 minutes at 200°C (400°F). Now warm up the spinach soup and whisk with a hand blender.

❹ Before serving, arrange the crêpes on the center of the plates, top with the blanched spring onions and pour some spinach soup around them.

Vegetarian Cuisine

Sacher

Porcini Mushrooms
with herbs au gratin

INGREDIENTS

10 porcini mushrooms, cleaned
4 shallots, finely diced
1 clove garlic, finely chopped
1 small bunch parsley, finely chopped
Olive oil
Salt, freshly ground pepper

POLENTA

120 g (1/2 cup) white polenta
1/2 liter (2 cups) vegetable stock
125 ml (1/2 cup) milk, 125 ml (1/2 cup) heavy cream
1 bay leaf
1 pinch nutmeg, freshly grated
Salt, freshly ground pepper

IN ADDITION

Butter flakes, parmesan, freshly grated
Garden herbs, plucked (chervil, parsley, cress, etc.)

❶ Put the vegetable stock in a pot and heat it up with the milk, the cream, as well as the bay leaf, nutmeg, salt and pepper. Gradually add the polenta and, constantly stirring, let it swell for about 30 minutes (the polenta should be soft and pliable).

❷ Thinly slice the mushrooms. Heat up the olive oil in a pan, fry the mushrooms golden brown; salt. Add the shallots, chopped garlic and parsley. Season and toss briefly.

❸ Distribute the mushrooms on a deep, heat-proof plate and cover with polenta. Sprinkle with grated parmesan and place butter flakes on top. Put into a preheated oven and gratinate at 220°C (425°F). Serve with sprinkled garden herbs.

TIP: "Polenta bianca," the white polenta, comes from Venice; it is somewhat finely spiced and is popular in Italy as a side dish to fish dishes. Here it is, as also common with the more well-known yellow polenta, combined with fried mushrooms.

Vegetarian Cuisine

Sacher

72

Bohemian Mushroom Goulash

Yields 4–6 portions

INGREDIENTS

**400 g (6 cups) mixed seasonal
mushrooms (porcini, bay bolete,
chanterelles, etc.)
300 g (10.5 oz.) floury potatoes
100 g (3.5 oz.) carrots
100 g (3.5 oz.) celery root
1 bunch spring onions
150 g (5.2 oz.) shallots
1 bunch parsley
1 sprig lovage
750 ml (3 cups) vegetable stock
150 ml (5 fl. oz.) dry white wine
2–3 tbsp must vinegar, seasonal
150 g (5.2 fl. oz.) sour cream,
60 g (2.1 oz.) butter
1 bay leaf
1 sprig lovage, 5 juniper berries
1 tbsp paprika, sweet
1 pinch caraway seeds, ground
White pepper, freshly ground
Salt**

❶ Clean the mushrooms and cut them into sufficiently sized pieces. Wash and clean the carrots, celery root and spring onions; peel the potatoes. Cut everything into small cubes. Peel the shallots and chop finely. Heat the butter in a pot and sweat the shallots; stir in the paprika powder and immediately pour in the white wine. Add the potatoes, carrots, celery root and spring onions and pour in the stock. Add the bay leaf, juniper berries, caraway seeds, salt and pepper. Bring to the boil and boil vigorously for 10–15 minutes – until the liquid is thick. Then add the mushrooms, mix in well and simmer for another 5 minutes. Remove the bay leaf and juniper berries from the mushroom goulash.

❷ Finely chop the parsley and lovage. Stir the sour cream with 1-2 tablespoons of the goulash until smooth; mix with the parsley and lovage mix and add to the goulash.
Mix everything well, season with vinegar. Let stand for a few more minutes, then arrange on deep plates.

A CLASSIC SIDE DISH: bread dumplings (see p. 48).

Classic Krautfleckerl

(Cabbage pasta)

Yields 6 to 8 portions

INGREDIENTS
400 g (14 oz.) pasta
1 head of white cabbage
2 onions
10 tbsp shortening or oil
2 tbsp sugar
Some caraway seeds,
** ground**
Salt, freshly ground pepper

❶ Cook the pasta al dente in a large pot of salted water. Strain, douse with water; drain.

❷ Remove the stem of the cabbage; clean and divide into small squares. Put in a bowl and bruise it. Let sit for about 15 minutes. In the meantime, peel the onions and chop them finely. Then heat up the butter or oil, stir in the sugar and caramelize. Add the chopped onions; fry golden brown. Squeeze out the cabbage and fold into the onions; season with salt, pepper and caraway seeds. Then cover the pot and cook for approx. 30 minutes until soft – stirring from time to time.

❸ Combine the pasta and the cabbage mix; let cook for another 4-5 minutes; taste and season before serving.
Photo opposite page

Egg Dumplings

INGREDIENTS
Dumplings
4 eggs
1/2 bunch of chives,
** finely chopped**
2 tbsp shortening or butter
Nutmeg, freshly grated
Salt
Freshly ground pepper

❶ Prepare the dumpling batter and dumplings according to the recipe on page 48. Cook them in salted water. Strain, and douse with cold water and drain well in a strainer.

❷ Whisk the eggs and season with nutmeg, salt and pepper. Heat the shortening in a frying pan, add the dumplings and toss. Then pour the egg mass over the dumplings – leave to absorb for a maximum of 2 minutes.

TIP: The egg dumpling dish is typically served at Viennese taverns or pubs for those with a moderate hunger. If you like, you can also sweat 2 finely chopped shallots in butter before you add the dumplings.

CLASSIC SIDE DISH: lettuce salad.

Vegetarian Cuisine

Sacher

Fried Risotto Balls
with red bell pepper foam

INGREDIENTS

1 liter (4.2 cups) vegetable stock
200 g (7 oz.) risotto rice
    (Arborio or Carnaroli)
2 shallots, finely cubed
2 eggs
20 g (3 tbsp) parmesan,
    freshly grated
40 g (1.4 oz.) buffalo mozzarella,
    cut into small cubes
200 g (7 oz.) panko flour
    (from an Asian grocery)
1 tbsp dry white wine
30 ml (2 tbsp) olive oil
Salt

RED BELL PEPPER FOAM

400 g (14 oz.) red bell pepper,
    seeded, finely cubed
1 shallot, finely cubed
125 ml (1/2 cup) vegetable stock
125 g (1/2 cup) heavy cream
80 g (2.8 oz) butter
Salt
Freshly ground pepper

IN ADDITION

Chervil leaves for the garnish

❶ For the risotto, boil the vegetable stock in a pot and add salt. Reduce the heat (but keep the stock hot). Heat the oil in a casserole; sweat the shallots lightly. Add the rice and sauté until it is transparent. Now, using a soup ladle, take approx. 1/8 liters (1/2 cup) of the hot vegetable stock and slowly pour in and stir – let evaporate. Now, ladle by ladle, add some vegetable stock and meanwhile, keep stirring the risotto. After 20 minutes, the stock should all be used up, all the liquid evaporated, and the risotto should be done. Shortly prior to the end of the cooking time, slowly stir in the white wine and grated parmesan. Finally, remove the rice from the stove and let cool.

❷ Afterward, divide the cooled risotto into 8 equal portions. Form each portion into one small, provisional ball. Place each of these balls one by one onto the palm of your hand and flatten it, placing in the middle a few cubes of mozzarella as a filling, then close the risotto mass from the edge and roll into a ball between your palms. This way, you should be able to form 8 nice, round risotto balls filled with mozzarella. Then pour some panko flour onto a plate and spread it around a little. Crack both the eggs onto a deep plate and beat them. Now bread the risotto balls – first placing them in the eggs and then rolling them in the panko flour. Pat well all around.

❸ For the red pepper foam, heat up the butter in a pot, add the prepared shallot and cubed peppers and sweat. Pour in some vegetable stock. A little later, add the cream and reduce the liquid to about half. Blend in the mixer and put through a sieve. Salt and pepper to taste, and foam it with a hand blender.

❹ Finally, heat up some oil in an appropriate pot and fry the rice balls for approx. 2 minutes until golden brown. Remove the balls from the oil with a strainer ladle and drain on kitchen paper.

❺ Pour some of the foam on each plate and place 2 rice balls on top. Garnish with chervil.

TIP: As an alternative to the red bell pepper foam you can also serve a tomato sauce or creamed spinach with the risotto balls.

Vegetarian Cuisine

Le 29. 10. 99

Huitres
Bouillon
Truites bleu s.ce hollande
Boeuf bouilli garni
Faisans flanqué
Des Cailles
Salade - Compotes
Parfait au chocolat
Fruits
fromage

Alexandre

Main Dishes with Fish & Meat

Zander from Neusiedl Lake
with vegetable-cream cabbage and bacon potatoes

INGREDIENTS

4 zander filets (with skin)
150 g (5.3 oz.) each
1 clove garlic, crushed
2 sprigs thyme
Olive oil
Salt
Freshly ground pepper

FISH SAUCE

200 ml (0.8 cup) sauce vin
blanc (see p. 85)
1 tbsp mustard seeds,
blanched

VEGETABLE-CREAM-CABBAGE

1 small white cabbage head
1 bunch of root vegetables,
peeled
2 shallots
1 tbsp chives, finely cut
1 tbsp pearl barley
100 ml (3.4 fl. oz.) heavy
cream
1 tbsp crème fraîche
50 g (1.7 oz.) shortening

BACON-POTATOES

12 small potatoes, boiled
and peeled
12 slices streaky bacon
2–3 sprigs rosemary
Shortening

❶ For the vegetable-cream-cabbage, halve the cabbage head and cut off the stem. Then cut the cabbage into small, diamond-shaped pieces, blanch in salted water and douse with ice water. Also cut the root vegetables into small, diamond-shaped pieces and blanch. Blanch the barley. Peel and finely cube the shallots. Heat the shortening in a pot and sweat the shallots. Add the blanched barley, cabbage and root vegetables, then stir in the heavy cream and the crème fraîche. Simmer until the cabbage and vegetables are cooked. Season with salt and pepper. Finely chop the chives and fold them in.

❷ Blanch a tablespoon of mustard seeds. Prepare a sauce vin blanc (see p. 85); add the mustard seeds.

❸ For the bacon potatoes, wrap each of the small, boiled and peeled potatoes in a slice of bacon. Heat some shortening in a pan, add rosemary sprigs and fry the potatoes until crispy.

❹ Season the zander, and first, fry the skin-side down in a pan with hot olive oil until crispy, then turn the filets over, add garlic, butter and thyme to the pan and fry until done.

❺ Whisk the prepared sauce vin blanc with a hand blender. Arrange the vegetable cabbage on the center of the plates; place the perch on top. Put three potatoes on each plate and pour over some sauce.

BY THE WAY: Zander ("fogasch" in Hungarian), a fish from the perch family, is the undisputed king of the Neusiedl Lake. Fishing has a long tradition here and the art is passed down from generation to generation. Because the lake is somewhat like a bath tub in summer, it's too warm for the salmonids (trout, char, etc.). So the perch has found its refuge here and is a popular delicacy, with its white, delicate meat.

Poached Rainbow Trout
with wild garlic and potato purée

INGREDIENTS
4 brook trout filets
250 ml (1 cup) fish stock
125 ml (1/2 cup) white wine
2 bay leaves
Peppercorns and cilantro seeds
1 bouquet garni (see Tip)
Salt, freshly ground pepper

IN ADDITION
125 ml (1/2 cup) sauce vin blanc
150 g (5 oz.) wild garlic, blanched and pressed
400 g (2 cups) potato purée
1 small glass of trout caviar

FOR THE SAUCE VIN BLANC
400 ml (13.5 fl. oz.) fish stock
1–2 shallots
100 ml (3.4 fl. oz.) white wine
3 cl (6 tsp) vermouth (Noilly Prat)
1 squeeze lemon juice
1/4 liter (1/2 cup) heavy cream
2 tbsp butter for sautéing
Cayenne pepper
Salt, freshly ground pepper

❶ First, blanch the wild garlic and pat dry. Prepare the potato purée according to the recipe on page 47 and keep warm.

❷ Then boil the fish stock and white wine with the bay leaves, a few peppercorns and cilantro seeds and the bouquet garni and steep. Season the trout filets with salt and pepper, then carefully place in the stock and gently poach.

❸ For the sauce vin blanc, finely chop the shallots. Heat up the butter in a pan and sauté the shallots. Deglaze with white wine and Noilly Prat. Let boil and reduce until there's hardly any liquid left. Then pour in the fish stock. Bring to the boil again and reduce the stock to about 1/3 (generous indication). Then, stir in the cream and let simmer for another 5 minutes. Strain through a strainer and season with pepper, cayenne pepper, salt and lemon juice. Bring the finished sauce to the boil once more; add the blanched wild garlic and blend everything using a hand mixer.

❹ Before serving, arrange the potato purée on plates, pour around some sauce. Place the trout filets in the middle of the plate. Garnish with caviar.

TIP: A bouquet garni is a bundle of herbs used in the preparation of soups, stocks, etc., and which is then removed. Simply gather together some fresh herbs like estragon, rosemary, thyme, dill and/or other similar herbs (you can also include bay leaves or cloves). Bind it together using kitchen twine.

Huchen · Danube Salmon

with Brussels sprouts and calf's tongue

INGREDIENTS

600 g (1.3 pounds) salmon
1 sprig thyme
Olive oil
Butter
Salt, freshly ground pepper

TONGUE AND BRUSSELS SPROUTS VEGETABLES

1 calf's tongue
250 ml (1 cup) stock from the tongue (veal stock)
500 g (18 oz.) Brussels sprouts
1 bunch herbs and vegetables for making soup
2 tbsp colorful cubed vegetables (carrots, turnip, celery root, leek)
1 tbsp parsley, chopped
Cornstarch for binding
2 tbsp cold butter
Bay leaf
A few peppercorns
Salt
Freshly ground pepper

IN ADDITION

400 g (2 cups) potato purée (see p. 47)
1 tbsp wasabi paste
Some horseradish, freshly grated

❶ For the Brussels sprouts vegetables with calf's tongue, boil some water in a pot and cook the tongue, continuously skimming off the foam. Wash the herbs and vegetables and add to the pot together with the bay leaf and peppercorns. Once the tongue is done, remove it and place briefly in iced water. While still warm, remove the skin. Cut into small cubes.

❷ Prepare the potato purée according to the recipe on page 47 – put the potatoes on now. Then purée during the next preparation stages (still before the fish) and keep warm, if necessary.

❸ Clean the Brussels sprouts and pluck off individual leaves; blanch in salted water and douse in ice water. For the cubed vegetables, cube and blanch some peeled carrots, turnip, celery root and leek.

❹ Heat up the stock and bind it with butter; add the vegetable cubes, Brussels sprouts, tongue and chopped parsley and season. Cut the filets into four equal pieces; season with salt and pepper. Heat up the olive oil in a pan, place the fish, skin side down into the pan and fry until crispy; turn over and add butter and thyme; fry until done. Season the potato purée with wasabi.

❺ Before serving, spread the purée on the middle of a plate and cover with the tongue-Brussels sprout-vegetables; place a filet on each plate and sprinkle with freshly grated horseradish.

BY THE WAY: Huchen – also known as Danube salmon – comes from the salmon family (salmonids) and is considered to be the king of sweet-water fish. Not only due to its impressive size (it's not uncommon for salmon to weigh more than 30 kg (67 pounds). Due to the fact that its natural habitat is rapidly dwindling, it's most often only available through fish farms. One of the last remaining bodies of water in which the salmon still lives and can be caught is, for example, the Drava River in Carinthia.

Wells Catfish in Root Stock

with caraway-seed potatoes

INGREDIENTS

800 g (1.8 pounds) catfish filet (Wels), 4 pieces of 200 g (7 oz.) each, deboned
100 g (3.5 oz.) celery root, peeled
1 carrot, peeled
1/2 leek, only the white part
1 small onion
Juice from 1/2 lemon
200 ml (7 fl. oz.) fish stock, 100 ml (3.4 fl. oz.) white wine
100 ml (3.4 fl. oz.) white wine vinegar
1 tbsp butter
Horseradish, freshly grated
1 bay leaf, 1 sprig thyme
2 cloves, 1 tsp sugar, salt

IN ADDITION

1 clove garlic, peeled
1kg (2.2 pounds) potatoes, peeled
Chives, chopped, for sprinkling
1 tbsp caraway seeds, whole

❶ Put the white wine, vinegar and fish stock together with salt and a teaspoon of sugar in a large pot and boil. Add the bay leaf, thyme and cloves and simmer. Finely chop the half onion and cut the carrot, celery root, leek into fine strips. Put the onion in the stock and bring to the boil again. Put the fish in another suitably sized pot and pour over the stock; place on the stove and let steep over low heat for about 10 minutes until they are done. Shortly before the filets are finished, add the vegetable strips.

❷ Peel and quarter the potatoes (cutting bigger potatoes into smaller pieces, if necessary) and boil in a pot with salted water and the caraway seeds until soft.

❸ Once the filets are cooked, remove from the stock and keep warm. Strain the stock and put the vegetables in a bowl (or a deep plate) and keep warm. Bring the stock to the boil again and reduce the heat; stir in the cold butter. Finish by adding some lemon juice. Strain the potatoes.

❹ Before serving, distribute the root vegetables on the middle of prewarmed plates. Arrange the potatoes decoratively beside the vegetables. Place one filet per plate on the vegetables; pour over some stock and garnish with horseradish and chives.

Main Dishes with Fish

Sacher

"Spring" Brook Trout

with morels, asparagus and wild garlic

INGREDIENTS

4 brook trout filets
12 morels, cleaned
1 clove garlic
1 sprig thyme
Butter
Salt
Freshly ground pepper

SPRING VEGETABLES

8 white asparagus (from the Marchfeld)
1 stale bread roll
Some sugar and lemon juice
4 green asparagus tips, washed
2 early potatoes, boiled, peeled, cubed
80 g (1/2 cup) fresh peas, blanched
4 baby carrots with the green, blanched and chopped into thirds
1 small kohlrabi (turnip), cubed and blanched
2 white icicle radishes, blanched and chopped into thirds
2 radishes, finely grated
Butter for tossing

WILD GARLIC BISCUITS

120 g (4.2 oz.) wild garlic
120 g (4.2 oz.) egg yolks (need to be weighed)
80 g (2.8 oz.) egg whites (need to be weighed)
1/2 clove garlic, chopped
Salt, freshly ground pepper
3 plastic cups

HERB OIL

1 tbsp mixed herbs, chopped
1 clove garlic, peeled
5 tbsp olive oil
Juice from 1 lemon

IN ADDITION

Spring herbs for the garnish (chervil, yarrow, chive blossoms, pimpernel, etc.)

❶ Peel the white (Marchfeld) asparagus, cut off the woody ends and then blanch in salted water with an old bread roll, some sugar and lemon juice. Prepare the rest of the vegetables (potatoes, green asparagus tips, baby carrots, kohlrabi, icicle radishes, radishes and peas) as described in the ingredients list.

❷ For the wild garlic biscuits, wash and drain the wild garlic and blend until you have about one tablespoon of wild garlic paste. Now fill a whipped cream dispenser with the paste and the remaining ingredients – egg yolk, egg white and the chopped garlic – and refrigerate for three hours. Then put 3 chargers in the cream dispenser and shake. Half-fill the three plastic cups with the wild garlic-egg mixture and put the cups in the microwave for 30 minutes. Then, turn the biscuits over and pull into the desired form. Put on a plate and put aside.

❸ For the herb oil, mix together the olive oil and lemon juice, chopped garlic and herbs.

❹ Season the trout filets with salt and pepper. Melt the butter in a frying pan, gently poach with the thyme and garlic (carefully let steep, not above 95°C/200°F). Add the cleaned, washed morels and continue poaching. Melt butter in a frying pan, add the prepared vegetables and toss briefly. Before serving, place the trout filets on the middle of the plate and cover with vegetables; distribute the wild garlic biscuit over the top. Dribble over some herb oil and decorate with the spring herbs.

Sea Bass

████ with Mediterranean vegetables and basil risotto

INGREDIENTS

4 slices of sea bass,
   150 g (5.3 oz.) each
1 clove garlic, pressed
1 sprig rosemary
Olive oil
Salt, freshly ground pepper

VEGETABLES

4 small zucchinis with
   blossom
2 mini eggplants
1 yellow bell peppers, peeled
1 red bell pepper
4 mushroom heads
2 beef tomatoes, peeled
8 baby artichokes, marinated
1 clove garlic, pressed
1 sprig rosemary
1 sprig thyme
1 bunch basil
Olive oil for grilling
Oil for frying

FOR THE BASIL RISOTTO

400 g (2 cups) risotto rice
   (Arborio or Vialone)
900 ml (4 cups) chicken or
   vegetable stock
1 shallot, small
40 g (6.5 tbsp) parmesan,
   freshly grated
125 ml (1/2 cup) dry white
   wine
50 g (1.7 oz.) butter
4 tbsp olive oil
1 pinch of saffron
Salt
3 tbsp basil, finely chopped
4 tbsp basil pesto

❶ For the vegetables, cut the blossoms off the 4 small zucchinis; blanch in salted water and douse with iced water. Cut the zucchinis in half lengthwise; cut the small eggplant in half. Peel the yellow bell pepper using a vegetable peeler; cut off the tops and bottoms, remove the core and then cut the bell peppers in quarters and triangles. Clean the mushrooms using a damp cloth. Quarter and de-seed the tomatoes. Cut the baby artichokes in half; wash, dry, then pluck the basil.

❷ For the basil risotto, heat some olive oil in a frying pan; finely chop the shallot and sauté. Now gradually sprinkle in the risotto rice, stirring, and sauté. As soon as the rice is transparent, deglaze with a glass of white wine and boil until the wine has totally evaporated. Then slowly, constantly stirring, pour in the stock – best done ladle by ladle. In the next 18 to 20 minutes, cook the risotto over low heat, stirring constantly. Now add the saffron. As soon as the rice is al dente, stir in the cold butter and freshly grated parmesan; season with salt. Remove the pot from the stove and, covered, let sit for approx. 1 minute. At the end, stir in 3 tablespoons of finely chopped basil.

❸ Heat up some olive oil in a grilling pan; add the herb sprigs and the pressed garlic, then the vegetables and the mushrooms and gently grill until soft. Season with salt and pepper.

❹ In a pot, heat up some oil, fry the prepared basil leaves and zucchini flowers and drain on some kitchen paper.

❺ For the fish, heat up some oil in a pan. Season the sea bass and first fry crispy on the skin side, turn over and finish frying with butter, garlic and the sprig of rosemary.

❻ Before serving, distribute the vegetables loosely on a plate, dribble over some pesto and place the risotto in the middle. Arrange the sea bass on the risotto, garnish with the fried basil leaves and some zucchini flowers. Dribble over some olive oil.

Main Dishes with Fish

Backhendl "Anna Sacher"
'Anna Sacher' Fried Chicken

INGREDIENTS

2 young, oven-ready chickens approx. 1 kg (2 pounds) each
4 chicken livers
1 bunch parsley
1 lemon, cut in slices
4 eggs, beaten
Breadcrumbs for breading
Flour for breading
Oil or schmaltz for frying
Salt

❶ Divide each chicken into 6 pieces - 2 wings, 2 legs and 2 breasts. To do this, use a sharp knife to cut off the wings. Then pull the legs outward and cut through the skin between the thigh and the breast, wiggling it until you find where the thigh meets the socket in the back; cut through the joint and repeat with the other leg. Then, hold the chicken with the neck facing upward and use a large knife to separate the breast cage from the back. To cut the breast in half, place the chicken, skin-side down on a chopping board and separate at the breast bone. If you want to cut each chicken into 8 pieces, now cut the breast in half again (crosswise). If desired, you can use a small knife to loosen the bones from the legs. But remember that a classic fried chicken is cooked with the bones still in the legs and the breast halves (or quarters).

❷ Now remove the skin from all the chicken pieces. Bread each piece, covering it with salt and then in flour, then in the beaten eggs and, finally, in the breadcrumbs. In a deep frying pan, fry the breaded chicken pieces in sufficient oil or schmaltz until golden brown – only turning once, if possible. After about 20–30 minutes, the chicken should be done.

❸ After approx. 12-15 minutes, bread the livers, add to the chicken and fry until done. Then take the crispy chicken pieces out of the oil and let drain on kitchen paper. In the meantime, put the parsley in the frying pan and fry in the rest of the hot oil.

❹ Arrange the chicken pieces on plates, placing one piece of liver on each plate; garnish with lemon slices and fried parsley. Good side dishes to go with Viennese fried chicken are lettuce, potato, or mayonnaise salad or parsley potatoes. Less traditional – and also especially popular – is the combination of potato-cornsalad salad with Styrian pumpkinseed oil (see p. 52).

TIP: You can keep the non-cooked chicken pieces, such as the back and neck, to use for chicken stock or soup.

Stuffed Corn-Fed Chicken Breast
with asparagus risotto

INGREDIENTS
**4 chicken breasts
with skin
2 sprigs rosemary;
shortening
Salt, freshly ground
pepper**

STUFFING
**200 g (7 oz.) chicken
60 g (2.1 oz.) goose
liver
2 tbsp pistachios,
chopped, lightly
roasted
2cl (4 tsp) white port
wine, 2 cl (4 tsp)
brandy
200 ml (0.8 cup) heavy
cream
Salt, freshly ground
pepper**

ASPARAGUS RISOTTO
**Risotto (see p. 79/91)
8 pieces of Marchfeld
asparagus
8 pieces of green
asparagus
1 tbsp mascarpone
1 stale bread roll
Juice from 1/2 lemon
1 pinch sugar**

SAUCE
**150 ml (5 fl. oz.)
chicken juice
2 tbsp balsamic
vinegar**

IN ADDITION
**Chervil for the
garnish**

❶ Peel both the white and green asparagus and cut off the lower woody ends (especially the white asparagus). Blanch the green asparagus in salted water. Together with the bread roll, some lemon juice and a pinch of sugar, also blanch the white asparagus in salted water. Put the asparagus aside for later.

❷ For the stuffing, cube the well-cooled chicken and, using a blender, blend together with the goose liver, brandy, port wine and cream. Season with salt and pepper and stir in the pistachios. Put into a pastry bag and refrigerate.

❸ Now cut the tips off the blanched asparagus and put aside for the garnish; cut the remaining asparagus into small pieces. Prepare the risotto. At the end, mix in the asparagus pieces and complete by adding the mascarpone. Keep the risotto warm.

❹ Pull back the skin of the chicken breasts slightly and, using the pastry bag, squeeze the filling under the skin (distribute as equally as possible). Then season the breasts with salt and pepper. Heat up the shortening in a frying pan and fry the chicken breasts, first on the skin side, then turn them over and finish frying with a sprig of rosemary.

❺ Warm up the asparagus tips. Heat up the chicken juice; season with balsamic, salt and pepper.

❻ Finally, place the risotto on deep plates, cut open the chicken breasts and arrange on the risotto, decorating with the asparagus tips. Pour over some juice and garnish with chervil.

Paprika Chicken

INGREDIENTS

2 small oven-ready chickens
    approx. 700–800 g
    (1.5 pounds or more) each
Approx. 300 ml (1.3 cups)
    chicken stock or water
150 g (5.3 oz.) onions
1/2 sour apple
Juice and grated zest from
    1/2 untreated lemon
If desired, 1/2 chili, deseeded,
    finely chopped
Some tomato paste
1/8 liter (1/2 cup) white wine
40 g (5 tbsp) fine flour
150 ml (5 fl. oz.) heavy cream
200 ml (0.8 cup) sour cream
Oil or shortening for frying
2 tbsp paprika powder, sweet
Salt
Freshly ground pepper

❶ First, peel and finely chop the onions. Then quarter each chicken (using chicken shears or a sharp knife, cut the wings off and cut the chicken into 4 pieces: 2 legs, 2 breasts; remove the backbone and the neck, if necessary). If the chicken is fatty, also pull off the skin. Wash the chicken pieces and pat dry with kitchen paper. Rub with salt. In a pot, heat the oil or butter and fry the chicken, but not too long – the meat should still have a light color. Then remove.

❷ Now, put the finely chopped onions in the pot. In the frying oil, fry the chicken golden brown. First add the tomato paste, then the paprika powder and immediately pour in the white wine. Stir well; top up with the stock. Add the bay leaf; season with salt and pepper, grated lemon rind as well as the finely chopped chili (leave out the chili, if desired). Bring to the boil and add first the legs – including the back, if you don't want to use it for anything else – and steam for about 20 minutes. Then add the breast pieces and stew for another 20 minutes, covered, until the meat is tender. Stir every now and then, adding some stock or water if necessary (the meat should always be covered with liquid). Finally, remove the meat from the stock (dispose of the backbone) and keep warm. Remove the bay leaf.

❸ Stir both creams with the flour until smooth and add to the stock; stir well. Peel and chop the half apple and add to the stock. Simmer everything, then, using a hand blender, purée and strain through a strainer. Pour into a pot and add the chicken legs and breasts, and then reheat. Arrange on prewarmed plates and serve with dumplings (recommended – see page 48).

TIP: The amount of chili you add alters the level of spiciness of the paprika chicken. To make the chicken more tender you can separate the bones from the breast and then, later, approx. 8–10 minutes prior to the end of cooking time, add the breasts to the chicken legs.

Main Dishes with Meat · Poultry

Farmer's Duck
with semolina dumplings and Champagne cabbage

INGREDIENTS

1 duck approx. 2 kg (4.4 pounds), oven-ready
1 sour apple
2 onions
1 sprig marjoram, fresh
1 sprig savory, fresh
300 ml (1.3 cups) chicken stock
50 ml (1.7 fl. oz.) sweet wine
Cornstarch, if necessary
1 pinch caraway powder
Salt
Freshly ground pepper

CHAMPAGNE CABBAGE

500g (18 oz.) mild sauerkraut, washed
300ml (1.3 cups) Champagne or dry sparkling wine
1/2 baby pineapple, peeled
1 small potato, peeled
1 onion, peeled
1 tbsp duck fat
1 bay leaf
5 juniper berries
1 clove
Sugar
Salt

SEMOLINA DUMPLINGS

see p. 49

❶ Preheat the oven to 180°C (350°F). For the duck stuffing, peel the apple and one of the onions and cut into small cubes. Pluck the marjoram and savory. In a bowl, mix the apple and onion cubes with the marjoram and savory leaves and pepper. Wash the duck inside and out; dry it, and rub with salt and pepper. Place the stuffing in the cavity and sew together using kitchen yarn (or pin together with wooden skewers).

❷ Peel and slice the second onion. Fill a large roasting pan about a finger deep with water; add the onion slices and place the duck on top, breast-side down. Put into a preheated oven and, at 180°C (350°F) roast for about 1 hour and 40 minutes, continually basting with the juices, until it is crispy.

❸ When the duck is done, scoop out the fat, collect the roast residue and put into a pan and heat it up. Deglaze with sweet wine, pour in chicken stock and reduce to about half the liquid. Add approx. 200 ml (0.8 cup) water and let simmer for 10 minutes, then strain and season. Possibly bind with cornstarch dissolved in water.

❹ Prepare the dumplings and make sure that they are finished to coincide with the roasting of the duck (if need be, let them steep in the hot water a bit longer).

❺ For the Champagne cabbage, peel the baby pineapple and cut into pieces; purée with a blender. Put the sauerkraut, Champagne, pineapple purée and 300 ml (1.3 cups) water in a pot and heat up. Stud the peeled onion with the clove and the bay leaf, place on the cabbage and add the juniper berries. Cover, and let simmer for about 30 minutes. Then remove the onion and grate the raw, peeled potato immediately into the cabbage, stir in and let simmer a further 5 minutes simmer. Season with salt, sugar and duck fat.

Sacher

Wiener Schnitzel
with parsley potatoes and mixed salad

INGREDIENTS

**8 veal cutlets approx. 90 g
(3 oz.) each
4 eggs
200 g (7 oz.) breadcrumbs,
very finely ground
100 g (3.5 oz.) fine flour
100 ml (3.4 fl. oz.) vegetable
oil
50 ml (1.7 fl. oz) shortening
Lemon slices
Salt**

❶ Tenderize the cutlets to about 2–4 mm (0.08-0.16 inches) and salt on both sides. On a flat plate, stir the eggs briefly with a fork (the egg becomes too thin if you beat them too long). First, coat the meat in flour, then in the beaten eggs and finally roll in the breadcrumbs.

❷ In a large frying pan, heat the shortening and oil (allow the fat to get really hot) and place the schnitzel in it. Fry golden brown, turn over and once again, fry golden brown. Keep swiveling the pan slightly so that the schnitzel is surrounded by fat and so that the breading becomes "fluffy." Remove, and drain on kitchen paper. Place the schnitzels on a warmed plate and serve garnished with slices of lemon.

TIPS: Make sure to use high-quality, very fine breadcrumbs. Genuine Wiener Schnitzels need to be fried in a frying pan, not in a deep fryer. Also, the use of butter is essential to give the schnitzels a typical "nutty" taste.

Main Dishes with Meat · Veal

Sacher

Creamy Veal Goulash
with dumplings

INGREDIENTS

1 kg (2.2 pounds) veal shoulder
200 g (7 oz.) onions
1 sour apple, peeled
Juice from 1 lemon
Some grated lemon zest
1 tbsp tomato paste
125 ml (1/2 cup) water
20 g (2.5 tbsp) flour
250 ml (1 cup) heavy cream
125 ml (1/2 cup) sour cream
4 tbsp oil
1 tsp paprika powder, sweet
1 tsp "rosen" paprika (hot)
1 bay leaf
Salt, freshly ground pepper

❶ Cut the meat into bite-size cubes and finely chop the onions. Heat the oil in a casserole dish and sauté the chopped onions until light brown. Add the tomato paste and paprika powder and deglaze with approx. 125ml (1/2 cup) water. Add the meat and enough water to just cover the meat. Add the bay leaf, salt and pepper and stew for about 1 1/2 hours. As soon as the meat is tender, remove again with a draining spoon.

❷ Remove the bay leaf. Grate the apple and stir in; add the lemon juice and rind. Mix in the flour, cream and sour cream. Bring to the boil, then mix with a hand-held mixer. Strain the liquid and add the meat and warm up briefly. Season with salt and pepper.

❸ For the dumplings, see recipe on p. 48.

Stuffed Breast of Veal
Viennese style

INGREDIENTS

1 breast of veal, approx. 3 kg
   (6.6 pounds) pocketed
Bones from the breast, finely
   chopped
1/2 liter (2 cups) veal juice
1 tbsp parsley, chopped
6 eggs
400 g (14 oz.) Kaisersemmeln
   – type of white bread roll,
   cubed
1/2 liter (2 cups) milk
100 g (3.5 oz.) melted butter
Butter for frying
Nutmeg, ground
Salt
Freshly ground pepper

❶ Wash the veal breast inside and out and pat dry with kitchen paper. If necessary, widen the pocket opening by hand or with a cooking spoon. Pour the milk into a bowl and soak the bread-roll cubes. Squeeze them out and mix well with melted butter, eggs and chopped parsley. Season with nutmeg, pepper and salt. Fill the veal breast with the stuffing using a spoon. Using a fist, push the mass firmly to the back of the cavity. Tightly sew the opening closed with thread. Rub the breast outside well with salt and pepper.

❷ Place the chopped bones into a baking dish and put the breast of veal, upside down, on top of the bones. Distribute some flakes of butter over the meat and roast in a preheated oven at 200°C (400°F) for about 15 minutes. Baste with the juice, then reduce the heat to about 160°C (320°F), and roast for another 30 minutes. Turn the breast over and roast for another 1 1/2–2 hours. Baste regularly, adding a little water if necessary.

❸ Remove the meat, wrap in greaseproof paper. Leave it to stand for at least 30 minutes in a warm place. Pour about 250 ml (1 cup) water into the meat juices, mixing in any residue from the dish and simmer well. Drain the fluid. Carve the meat, and place the slices on prewarmed plates with a little juice.

SUGGESTED SIDE DISHES: risipisi (rice and peas) or mashed potatoes.

TIP: The stuffing for the breast of veal is particularly tasty if you refine it with chopped chicken liver, briefly sautéed in butter and fried bacon, or also with peas and fried onions or cubed, pickled tongue, chopped black truffles and chopped roasted pistachios (or pine nuts).

Fried Veal Liver
Old-Viennese Style

ZUTATEN

800 g (1.8 pounds) veal liver
200 g (7 oz.) bacon, cut
in fine strips
250 g (8.8 oz.) small mushrooms
5–8 small shallots (for the
mushrooms)
3 tbsp finely chopped
shallots (for the liver)
400 ml (1.7 cups) veal juice
30 ml (2 tbsp) apple vinegar
Vegetable oil
Salt
Freshly ground pepper
Fresh marjoram, plucked
(Garnish)
Possibly some flour mixed
with butter
(for binding)

❶ Cut the cleaned mushrooms in slices. Also slice the shallots lengthways and sweat in hot oil. Add the mushrooms and brown them lightly. Add the bacon strips and fry together briefly. Season with salt and pepper and keep warm.

❷ Cut the cleaned veal liver (without membrane and veins) in thin slices and sear it in hot oil in a non-stick frying pan, while constantly swivelling the pan, but don't fry it through (the liver will otherwise become hard).

❸ Add the finely chopped shallots, sweat them and place the liver on a plate. Deglaze the pan residue with vinegar, pour over the veal juice and let it boil vigorously. Add the liver again; season with salt and pepper and, swiveling the pan vigorously, bind it with cold butter. If need be, stir in a little flour kneaded with butter, and bind the sauce with it.

❹ Arrange on prewarmed plates, sprinkle with the mushroom-bacon mixture and garnish with the plucked marjoram.

BY THE WAY: In Old-Viennese cuisine, veal liver was not served sprinkled with a mushroom-bacon mixture. Shortly before serving, the liver was refined with raisins soaked in sweet wine and pine nuts (or pistachios) roasted in butter and grated lemon peel.

Main Dishes with Meat · Veal

Sacher

Sirloin

with Onions, fried potatoes and gherkin mustard

INGREDIENTS

4 slices short loin
   approx. 180 g (6.3 oz) each
4 shallots
400 ml (13.5 fl. oz.) veal juice
200 ml (7 fl. oz) bouillon
100 ml (3.4 fl. oz.) vegetable oil
2cl (4 tsp) apple vinegar
Cold butter for binding
Flour
English mustard
Salt, freshly ground pepper

FRIED POTATOES

(see p. 47)

Gherkin mustard

❶ Clean the meat well and make small cuts into the top of the meat so that it doesn't bulge during frying, then tenderize with a meat hammer. Season with salt and pepper and spread with mustard. Dredge the meat on one side with flour. Heat the oil in a large frying pan. Brown the meat briefly on the floured side first, then, just as quickly, fry the other side. Remove from the frying pan and keep warm.

❷ Cut the shallots in strips, add to the frying pan and sauté until brown. Pour in the veal juice, apple vinegar and bouillon, and let the sauce boil. Stir in some butter to bind. Put the meat in a pot, pour over some sauce. Heat up and let steep well. Now prepare the potatoes (best done using parboiled potatoes).

❸ Arrange the meat on a plate, pour over some sauce and serve with potatoes. Serve the gherkin mustard separately.

Tafelspitz

(Boiled Beef with Classic Side Dishes)

INGREDIENTS

300 g (10.5 oz.) beef for
   boiling (first-cut flank,
   brisket or chuck)
300 g (10.5 oz.) beef marrow
   bones
350 g (12 oz.) root vegetables
   (parsnips, turnips, carrots
   and parsley root)
1 small bunch lovage
2 onions with skin
1 leek
Peppercorns, bay leaf
1 round of beef with a little
   fat, about 2 1/2-3 kg
   (5.5-6.5 pounds)
1 bunch chives
Salt
Freshly ground pepper
Fleur de Sel

MARROW BREAD

4 small slices rye bread
Freshly ground pepper
Fleur de Sel

❶ Press the marrow out of the beef bones and rinse them in cold water. Cut the meat into small cubes and place with the bones in cold water and blanch briefly. Then douse with cold water, put in a pot and cover with water. Slowly bring to the boil and constantly skim off the foam. Now add the round of beef and the herbs. Simmer just below boiling point over low heat for about 2-2 1/2 hours. Halve the unpeeled onion, and fry it, without fat, preferably in an old frying pan, on the cut surface until dark brown. An hour before the end of cooking, add the soup vegetables, leek, lovage and onions.

❷ Remove the cooked beef from the soup. Strain the soup using a straining cloth, and season. Slice the meat about a finger-width wide (against the grain) and put back in the soup to keep warm.

❸ Briefly poach the marrow slices in the hot soup, arrange them on slices of toasted rye bread and season with Fleur de Sel and ground pepper. Arrange the Tafelspitz on a warmed plate; if desired, add soup vegetables. Pour over a little soup. sprinkle with Fleur de Sel and chives.

❹ Classic side dishes: chive sauce, apple or bread-roll horseradish, creamed spinach, hash browns.

TIPS: When buying the meat, make sure that the cut of beef has a nice layer of fat. When cooking: as long as the meat is sitting in the soup, don't add salt, otherwise it will become red and dry. As is customary in Vienna, you can serve the soup before the beef, with one of the many Viennese soup garnishes (see recipes p. 34 ff).

Main Dishes with Meat · Beef

Sacher

Rindsrouladen · Beef Roulade

INGREDIENTS

8 rounds beef schnitzel (use ox meat)
    150 g (1/3 pound) each
2 tbsp hot English mustard
3 onions, cut lengthways
2 ripe tomatoes
1 bunch of vegetables for making
    soup, finely diced
200 ml (0.8 cup) Burgunder (or other
    heavy red wine)
1.2 l (5 cups) vegetable/beef stock
    or water
2 juniper berries, lightly pressed
1 bay leaf
1 vinegar pickle, finely chopped
Some grated lemon zest
40 ml (3 tbsp) vegetable oil for frying
Flour
Possibly cornstarch (Maizena)
Salt
Freshly ground pepper

IN ADDITION

Mashed potatoes, cooked as on
    page 47
Capers and sprigs of thyme for the
    garnish

STUFFING

2 carrots
1 turnip
1 bunch parsley, plucked
16 quail eggs (or 3 normal eggs)
8 slices prosciutto (or other cured
    ham)

FRIED ONIONS

2 white onions
Pinch paprika powder
50–100 g (1.8–3.5 oz.) flour, coarse
Peanut oil for frying
Salt

❶ Peel the carrots and turnip and cut thinly lengthways. Boil the quail eggs for 3 minutes, douse in cold water and peel carefully. Cover the beef pieces with plastic wrap and lightly tenderize. Season with salt and pepper, and spread mustard on one side. Cover first with prosciutto, then some vegetables (keep some for the sauce) and parsley. Place the eggs in the middle of the meat and tightly roll the fillet into a roulade. Pin it together with toothpicks. Season with salt and pepper, dust with flour and quickly fry all over in vegetable oil.

❷ Remove the beef and fry the chopped onions and the rest of the vegetables in the fat. Add the halved tomato and fry it, then deglaze with red wine. Add the bay leaf and berries, pour in the stock and place the roulade in the sauce. Roast in a preheated oven at 180°C (355°F) for 50–90 minutes (depending on the meat).

❸ While it's roasting, baste regularly. When the roulade is done, remove from the oven, and wrap it in foil. Keep warm. Add the finely-chopped pickle and lemon zest to the sauce and simmer vigorously. Strain the sauce, and season to taste. If it's too thin, add a little water and cornstarch. Place the roulade in the sauce and let it draw for about 10 minutes. Place the purée on hot plates, put the roulade on top and garnish with the fried onions, thyme and capers.

❹ For the fried onions, slice the onions with a bread slicer. Lightly salt them, sprinkle with paprika, and then coat in flour. Put into a coarse sieve and shake off the excess flour. Heat the oil in a frying pan and fry onions golden brown, turning frequently. Remove them, and drain on kitchen paper.

TIP: If you make the roulade with short sirloin, it cooks faster and is more tender.

Main Dishes with Meat · Beef

Suckling-Pig Cutlets
with cabbage and bacon potatoes

INGREDIENTS

1kg (2.2 pounds) saddle of suckling pig with rind
Pork schmaltz
300 g (2/3 pound) chopped bones
1 leek, coarsely chopped
2 onions
2 garlic cloves
1 small bottle dark beer
1/2 tsp caraway
Marjoram powder
Salt, freshly ground pepper

CABBAGE

1 small head of cabbage
1 red, 1 yellow bell pepper
2 tbsp blanched pearl barley
Salt and pepper
1 clove garlic, finely chopped
1 tbsp pork schmaltz

BACON POTATOES

16 small potatoes, washed and boiled al dente with skin
16 slices smoked streaky bacon

❶ Fill an appropriate frying pan with water about 2 fingers' deep and place in it the saddle of pork with the fat side down, and bring to the boil. Simmer for approx. 10 minutes.

❷ Afterward, make incisions in the fat corresponding with the desired thickness of the cutlets, and season with salt and pepper. Heat the schmaltz in the frying pan and fry the bones in it; add the leek, onions and garlic. Pour in the dark beer and add the herbs.

❸ Roast the pork in a preheated oven at 180°C (350°F) for approx. 50 minutes with the fat facing upwards and regularly baste with the juices. During the last 15 minutes, increase the heat to 220°C (425°F) and stop basting.

❹ Halve the cabbage and cut off the stem. Cut the individual leaves into diamond shapes and blanch in salted water. Peel the bell pepper, remove the core and also cut into diamond shapes. Heat up the schmaltz in a pot and sauté the pepper pieces. Add the finely chopped garlic and stir in the cabbage. Add a dash of water, the barley and season to taste.

❺ Let the roast stand in a warm place, strain the juices and season, possibly cooking it a bit longer. Divide the pork into the desired cutlet sizes.

❻ Wrap the potatoes in bacon, place in another frying pan and bake until crispy in the oven with the roast.

❼ Place the cabbage in the middle of a plate and pour sauce around. Decoratively position the cutlet and the potatoes around it.

TIP: The advantage of roasting the saddle whole is that the fat becomes even crispier!

Steirisches Wurzelfleisch
(Styrian Stewed Pork with Caraway Potatoes)

INGREDIENTS

8 waxy potatoes
1 kg (2.2 pounds) shoulder
of pork with fat
300 g (10.5 oz.) root
vegetables for soup
100 g (3.5 oz.) onions
1 bay leaf, 10 peppercorns
2 garlic cloves
Bunch of thyme
1/2 l (2 cups) water
Vinegar
Parsley, finely chopped
Horseradish, finely grated
Salt

❶ Quarter and peel the potatoes (they'll be cooked in the last 20 minutes with the stew)

❷ Wash the pork. Put the herbs in a linen bag and seal well. Peel the root vegetables and onions and cut into fine strips. Put the meat with the herbs, a little vinegar and the water in a pot and let simmer. When the meat is done, add the root vegetables and onions. If necessary, add liquid. Add the potatoes and cook everything until soft. Remove the herb bag and cut the meat into portions.

❸ Put the stock together with the vegetables in a soup bowl and distribute the meat and the potatoes in the soup. Garnish with horseradish and parsley.

TIP: According to taste, this classic of Austrian cuisine can also be prepared using lamb.

Rack of Lamb

with artichokes and potato chips

INGREDIENTS

600 g (1.3 pounds) rack of lamb with fat
Salt and ground pepper
Olive oil
2 sprigs thyme, 2 sprigs rosemary,
150 ml (5 fl. oz.) lamb juice

ARTICHOKES

16 small artichokes (Italian variety)
2 lemons
4 garlic cloves, 6 shallots
Olive oil

POTATO CHIPS

200g (7 oz.) potatoes, oil for frying

❶ Break off the artichoke stems, strip off the leaves, scrape off the fibrous "choke," cut off the bottom of the artichoke, and immediately put in lemon water, otherwise they'll turn brown. Peel shallots and garlic, heat the olive oil. Add the artichokes, shallots, thyme and garlic; season with salt and pepper and slowly braise in the oven (approx. 8 minutes at 170°C/340°F). Then keep warm.

❷ Season the lamb with salt and pepper and fry in a hot frying pan with olive oil. Add the rosemary and thyme and roast in the oven at 200°C (400°F) for 6 minutes; keep warm and let stand.

❸ Peel the potatoes and cut into cylinders 2 cm (0.8 inches) high. Using a vegetable cutter, slice off pieces and immediately put them in a bowl of water. Tip: So that the potato chips don't turn brown and thus the starch is not washed out, heat some oil in a casserole and fry the chips golden brown.

❹ Cut the rack of lamb into 4 portions. Place the artichokes on a plate and decoratively arrange the potato chips around them. Serve with lamb juice.

Roasted Venison
with celery root, mushrooms, broccoli and butter dumplings

INGREDIENTS

800 g (1.8 pounds) rack of venison (per person 200 g/7 oz.)
375 ml (1.5 cups) venison or beef stock
1 broccoli, cut in florets, blanched
10 small mushrooms, sliced, sautéed
1 tbsp cranberries
2 sprigs thyme, plucked
1 tbsp butter
Oil
Salt, freshly ground pepper
Black nuts (see tip p. 27) and rowan berries as garnish

CELERY ROOT PURÉE

Juice from 1/2 lemon
200 g (7 oz.) celery root (vitamin C !)
1 tsp ascorbic acid
50 g (3.5 tbsp) cold butter
Salt

BUTTER DUMPLINGS

200 g (7 oz.) butter
160 g (5.6 oz.) breadcrumbs (white bread)
4 eggs, 4 yolks
Nutmeg, freshly grated
Salt, freshly ground pepper

❶ For the butter dumplings, whisk the butter until white and foamy; gradually stir in the yolks, keep beating, and then slowly stir in the eggs. Add the breadcrumbs and season well with salt, pepper and nutmeg. Let stand briefly and then form dumplings; boil them in salted water.

❷ For the celery root purée, put the lemon juice and about 1/2 liter (2 cups) of water in a bowl. Peel the celery root, cut into small cubes and immediately put them in lemon water so that they stay nice and white. Boil 400 ml (13.5 fl. oz.) water with the ascorbic acid and some salt, add celery root, and cook until soft. Pat dry the still hot vegetables with kitchen paper, and, using a blender, finely purée with the butter. Pass through a sieve and season with salt.

❸ Clean the venison well and cut into large pieces and lightly tenderize. Season with salt and pepper, then coat the meat on one side with flour. Heat up the oil in a large frying pan. Sear the meat first on the floured side and then on the other side, and keep warm. Pour in the venison or beef stock and let boil. Add the cranberries and thyme and bind with the butter, then place the meat in the sauce.

❹ Blanch the broccoli (or, if already blanched, warm it up). Heat some oil in a frying pan; sauté the mushrooms, season with salt and pepper.

❺ Arrange the roast on prewarmed plates; nap with sauce. Put the celery root purée, broccoli, mushrooms and butter dumplings on top of the roast; garnish with thyme leaves, black nuts and rowanberries.

Sacher

Menu

du 24 Avril 1897.

Sévigné
Togas, sauce hollandaise
Boeuf braisé aux légumes
Homard à l'américaine en croûtes
Punch au Curaçao
Oisons nouveaux
Salade Romaine
Compotes
Asperges d'Argenteuil sauce vinaigrette
Crème glacée
Fruits
Fromages.

DRUCK VON A. REISSER, WIEN.

Sweet Sacher Recipes

Malakoff Torte

For a cake form of 24 cm (9 inches) Ø

INGREDIENTS

SPONGE BASE

5 eggs
120 g fine flour
150 g (5.2 oz.) superfine (caster) sugar
1 pkt. vanilla sugar
Grated zest from 1 untreated lemon
80 g (2.8 oz.) melted butter
40 g (1.4 oz.) cornstarch (Maizena)
1 pinch salt

VANILLA CREAM

2 egg yolks
2 eggs
100g (3.5 oz.) superfine (caster) sugar
1 pkt. vanilla sugar
Pulp from 1 vanilla bean, scraped out
500ml (2.1 cups) heavy cream
6 sheets gelatin, soaked in water
4cl (8 tsp) Amaretto

RUM SYRUP

150 g (5.2 oz.) superfine (caster) sugar
1/4 l (1 cup) rum
125 ml (1/2 cup) water

IN ADDITION

1 pkt. lady fingers
14 lady fingers
250 ml (1 cup) cream and slivered almonds for decoration

❶ Butter a spring form and sprinkle with flour. Preheat the oven. Then, for the sponge, in a bowl, beat the eggs, superfine sugar, vanilla sugar, salt and grated lemon zest in a warm bain-marie, then in a bain-marie with ice water. Sieve the flour and cornstarch. Gradually fold in the eggs. Slowly stir in the melted butter.

❷ Fill the cake form with the sponge mass and bake in a preheated oven at 180°C (350°F) for 30–35 minutes. Allow to cool. Remove the cake from the form and cut horizontally through the middle.

❸ Now for the vanilla cream, in a bowl, beat the eggs, egg yolk, sugar, vanilla sugar and vanilla pulp over in a warm bain-marie, then, in a bain-marie with ice water, until fluffy. Warm up the Amaretto. Pat dry the soaked gelatin sheets and dissolve in the Amaretto, then fold them into the egg mass. Whisk the cream until half stiff and fold it in.

❹ For the rum syrup, boil the water and sugar; allow to cool and add the rum. Pour into a bowl.

❺ Place one half of the 2 sponge cakes in a spring form and dribble over some rum syrup. Then spread about 2 cm (approx. 1 inch, or less) of vanilla cream over the cake. Dip the ladyfingers briefly in the rum syrup and place carefully them next to each other on top of the cream layer. Then spread another layer of the vanilla cream over the cake and smooth it over. Dip the lady fingers one after the other in the rum syrup and carefully place them on the cream next to each other. Spread another layer of vanilla cream, same thickness, over the ladyfingers and cover again with ladyfingers. And repeat. Now spread the rest of the cream over the cake and cover with the second sponge. Keep the cake cool overnight.

❻ Carefully remove the cake from the form. Beat 250 ml (1 cup) cream and cover the Malakoff Torte all around with the cream. You can possibly use the rest of the cream in a pastry bag and decorate the cake with a few pretty roses. Finish the decoration with the slivered almonds and the remaining 14 ladyfingers.

Sacher-Torte

INGREDIENTS

For a spring form of 22–24 cm (8-9 inches) Ø

140 g (4.9 oz.) fine flour
130 g (1 cup) dark chocolate
Approx. 200 g (7 oz.) apricot
  jam
110 g (3.9 oz.) confectioners'
  sugar
110 g (3.9 oz.) superfine
  (caster) sugar
Pulp from 1/2 vanilla bean,
  scraped out
6 egg yolks
6 egg whites
140 g (4.9 oz.) butter, room
  temperature
Butter and flour for the form
Heavy cream for decoration

FROSTING

150g (5.2 oz.) dark chocolate
200g (7 oz.) superfine (caster)
  sugar
125ml (1/2 cup) water

*Original
Sacher-Torte*

Since 1832, the
Original Sacher-Torte
has been produced
using a strictly kept
secret recipe. The
recipe presented here
is a variation of the
Sacher-Torte.

❶ Line the bottom of the cake form with baking paper and grease the sides of it with butter; dust with flour. Preheat the oven at 170°C (340°F).

❷ In a bowl, whip the butter, confectioners' sugar and vanilla pulp until creamy. Gradually add the egg yolks, and continue beating until the mixture is thick and creamy. Melt the chocolate in a bain-marie [water bath] (or microwave), then fold it into the butter-egg-yolk mass. Beat the 6 egg whites until stiff, sprinkling in the sugar, and continue to beat. When the mass is stiff and glossy, heap the beaten egg white onto the egg yolk mixture, then sift over the flour. Carefully fold everything with a cooking spoon. Fill the spring form with the mixture and place in a preheated oven. Bake for 55 to 60 minutes at 170°C (340°F), leaving the door slightly ajar during the first 10–15 minutes (use a cooking spoon to keep it open), then close the door and finish baking. (You can test the cake to see if it's done by pressing it lightly. If it's done, it should show slight resistance, then resume its form again, like a sponge).

❸ Then, turn the cake upside down on a cake rack in the spring form and allow to cool for about 20 minutes. Peel off the baking paper. Put the form back on the cake, then turn the cake over, and allow to fully cool in the form so that all the unevenness can settle and smooth out on the surface. Then, remove the cake form and cut the cake in half horizontally with a sharp knife. Carefully lift up the top half and place next to the bottom half of the cake.

❹ Warm up the jam, stir until smooth and spread onto both cake halves, then put it back together again. Spread the jam all over the cake and allow it to dry a little.

❺ In the meantime, for the frosting, bring the water and sugar to boil so that it bubbles for about 5–6 minutes. Allow to cool slightly. Break the chocolate into pieces and melt in a bain-marie and, stirring, gradually add the sugar and stir with an egg whisk. Keep stirring until you have a thick, smooth frosting.

❻ Quickly pour the slightly warm frosting over the cake in one movement. Using a spatula, spread the frosting smoothly over the surface of the cake with the fewest possible strokes. Smooth over. Let dry for a few hours (until the frosting is very solid). Finally, cut the Sacher-Torte into pieces and place on a plate. Serve with whipped cream.

TIP: For the SACHER desserts, we only use fine flour.

Esterházy Torte

1 cake of 24 cm (9 inches) Ø (14 pieces)

INGREDIENTS

THIN CAKE BASES
8 egg whites
Zest from 1 untreated lemon
150 g (5.2 oz.) ground almonds
40 g (1.4 oz.) fine flour
200 g (7 oz.) confectioners' sugar
Cinnamon, ground
Baking paper

BUTTER CREAM
300 g (10.5 oz.) soft butter
300 ml (1.2 cups) milk
150 g (5.2 oz.) sugar
40 g (1.4 oz.) vanilla custard powder
3 egg yolks
2 cl (4 tsp) cherry brandy
Pulp from 1 vanilla bean, scraped out
50 g (1.7 oz.) nougat, melted

FROSTING
300 g (10.5 oz.) fondant (thick, white sugar glaze)
80 g (2.8 oz.) apricot jam
2–3 tbsp slivered almonds, roasted
2 cl (4 tsp) rum
Cocoa powder

❶ For the cake bases, first, draw 6 circles of about 24 cm (9 inches) Ø on baking paper (incl. the cake hoop). Preheat the oven at 200°C (400°F). Grate the lemon zest. Whisk the egg white with the confectioners' sugar until stiff and glossy, also add the lemon zest and a pinch of cinnamon and stir in. Now sieve the flour, mix with the grated almonds, and carefully fold into the whites. Spread the cake mixture thinly over each of the 6 baking paper circles and immediately, one after the other (or in batches), bake in the oven for 8–10 minutes. Remove from the oven, and, with one of the cake rings placed on each of the cake bases, cut out exact circular shapes again. Loosen the bottom of each warm cake base from the paper with a spatula and allow to cool.

❷ Meanwhile, prepare the butter cream. In a small pot, heat 200 ml (0.8 cup) milk with the scraped out vanilla pulp and bring to the boil once. Use the rest of the 100 ml (3.4 fl. oz.) milk to mix with the egg yolk, vanilla custard powder and cherry brandy with an egg whisk and then stir into the hot milk. Stir until smooth (possibly pass through a sieve, should the custard have formed lumps). Allow to cool. Meanwhile, beat the butter until very creamy. Gradually stir the cooled custard into the creamy butter mixture. Mix half of the cream with the nougat.

❸ Put one nice, level cake base to one side. Spread the butter cream and nougat alternately over each of the other five cake layers and place them on top of each other, keeping some cream for the end. Put the 6th layer upside down (with the smooth bottom side facing up) on top of the cake. Heat the jam and rum and spread over the top of the cake. Refrigerate.

❹ For the frosting, warm the fondant to body temperature (i.e., lukewarm) and put aside 2 to 3 tablespoons of it. Spread the rest of the warm fondant over the layer of jam and smooth over with a spatula. Spread the sides of the cake with the rest of the butter cream using a spatula and apply the slivered roasted almonds to the sides of the cake (press lightly!). Evenly mix the 2 to 3 tablespoons of fondant with the cocoa and fill a pastry bag. Starting from the center of the cake moving outwards to the edge, squeeze out a spiral with about 5 to 6 lines and around 2 cm (approx 1 inch, or less) apart. Then, using a toothpick or a small knife (only touching the frosting), pull the toothpick from the center outwards (as if you were "cutting" the cake) into equal quarters so that each spiral line gets a "point" where they touch each other. Then, "half" the quarters of these cocoa-frosting lines – from the outside in – so that a large, spider-web-like net, which is typical for the Esterhazy Torte, is created on the frosting surface.

Sacher

Linzer Torte

For a cake form of 24 cm (9 inches) Ø

INGREDIENTS

BATTER

200 g (7 oz.) ground hazelnuts
200 g (7 oz.) butter
200 g (7 oz.) confectioners' sugar
100 g (3.5 oz.) fine flour
2 tbsp vanilla sugar
3 eggs
1 egg yolk
Grated zest from 1 untreated
    lemon
Grated zest from 1 untreated
    orange
2 pinches ground cinnamon
1 pinch cloves, ground
1 pinch salt
Butter for greasing
Flour for the work surface

COVERING

1 large wafer (20 cm/8 inches Ø)
    or several small ones
150 g (5.2 oz.) red currant jam
150 g (5.2 oz.) almonds, grated
Confectioners' sugar for
    sprinkling

❶ In a bowl, beat the butter and confectioners' sugar until creamy. Stir in the grated lemon and orange zest, cinnamon and clove powder. One after the other, fold in the three eggs and the egg yolks. Mix the cake crumbs, flour and grated hazelnuts together and combine well with the mass to make a batter.

❷ Grease the torte or spring form with butter, dust with flour. Fill with 2/3 of the batter; press it against the rim (if using a spring form, not too high). Now place the wafer (or wafers, if you are using several) on top of the batter and spread over some red currant jam.

❸ Fill the rest of the batter into a pastry bag with a smooth spout (size 6) and use it to decorate a lattice crust over the jam. Sprinkle with grated almonds, then place the Linzer Torte at 160–170°C (340°F) in a preheated oven bake for 45–50 minutes. Allow to cool. Sieve some confectioners' sugar over the top.

Marmorgugelhupf
(Marble Bundt Cake)

INGREDIENTS
200 g (7 oz.) butter
100 g (3.5 oz.)
confectioners' sugar
Some vanilla sugar
4 eggs
230 g (8.1 oz.) fine flour
100 g (3.5 oz.) superfine
(caster) sugar
20 g (4 tsp) cocoa
powder
Pinch of salt

❶ Beat the butter, confectioners' sugar and vanilla sugar and a pinch of salt until fluffy. Crack the eggs, separate the yolks and egg whites. Gradually stir the egg yolks into the butter mass. Whisk the egg whites with the sugar until stiff and fold into the egg yolk mixture. Sieve the flour and fold it in. Sieve the cocoa powder and combine it with 1/3 of the batter.

❷ Grease the bundt pan with butter, and dust with flour. Now fill the form with half the light mixture and then with dark, and then distribute the rest of the light batter over the top. Using a fork, move it in a spiral motion through the layers of batter, creating a marble pattern.

❸ Bake in a preheated oven at 180°C (350°F) for about an hour. Overturn the cake onto a cake rack and allow to cool. Sprinkle with confectioners' sugar.

Germgugelhupf
(Yeast Bundt Cake)

INGREDIENTS

70 g (2.5 oz.) raisins
40 ml (8 tsp) rum
2 eggs
6 yolks
350 g (0.8 pounds) flour
100 g (3.5 oz.) sugar
250 g (1/2 pound) soft
  butter
Butter for greasing
Sugar for dusting

FOR THE SPONGE MIXTURE

210 ml (7 fl. oz.)
  lukewarm milk
150 g (5.2 oz.) flour
1 cube yeast, fresh
60 g (2.1 oz.) sugar

❶ One or two days in advance, combine the raisins and rum and let draw for about 24 hours. Then, for the sponge mixture (the preferment), warm up the milk and pour it into a bowl when lukewarm. Crumble the yeast, add it to the milk and stir. Stir in the sugar and sieved flour, mixing everything well. Cover with a damp tea towel and leave to rise in a warm place for approx. 30 minutes.

❷ Afterward, for the dough, sieve 350 g (0.8 pounds) flour into a bowl and combine with the 2 eggs, 6 egg yolks, sugar, salt and vanilla sugar. Add the sponge mixture and knead in the soft butter. Knead the dough for approx. 10 minutes in a blender. At the end, fold in the rum-raisins. Cover the dough and let rise for about 30 minutes.

❸ Now, grease a bundt cake pan with butter and sprinkle with sugar. Place the dough inside, pressing it downwards. Leave to rise again – long enough so that the dough rises to about 2/3 its size. Then brush with butter and bake in a preheated oven at 160°C (320°F) for approx. 40–50 minutes. Allow to cool and turn over.

Apple Strudel

INGREDIENTS
1 strudel pastry, ready-made or self-made

FILLING
1.5 kg (3.3 pounds) apples, not too juicy (Elstar, Kronprinz Rudolf), peeled and cored
200 g (7 oz.) butter
100 g (3.5 oz.) superfine (caster) sugar
30 g vanilla sugar
60 g (2.1 oz.) raisins soaked in rum
100 g (3.5 oz.) breadcrumbs
1 pinch cinnamon
Butter for daubing
1 egg for daubing
Confectioners' sugar for dusting

❶ Use the recipe on p. 46 to prepare the strudel pastry. Place it on top of a tea towel dusted with flour and roll it out.

❷ For the filling, peel and quarter the apples, then cut into thin slices. Quickly dribble over some lemon juice (so they don't go brown). Put the rum-raisins and 2 tablespoons of sugar and half of the vanilla sugar in a bowl; add the apple slices and combine everything well.
Melt 200 g (7 oz.) butter in a small pan. Brush the strudel pastry with half of the melted butter. Use the rest of the butter to fry the breadcrumbs golden brown. Then combine the breadcrumbs with the rest of the sugar and vanilla sugar and a pinch of cinnamon and spread over 2/3 of the strudel. Don't cover the edges, about 3 cm (approx. 1 inch) from the edge on both sides. Distribute the apple filling equally on top of the breadcrumbs. Fold in the side edges and, using the tea towel, roll up the strudel (start with the side with the filling).

❸ Grease a baking tray with butter, or use baking paper. Beat the egg. Lift the strudel carefully with the towel and with the sealed side facing downwards, place on the tray. Brush with the beaten egg. Bake in a preheated oven at 180°C (350°F) for approx. 30–40 minutes, intermittently brushing with the melted butter. Allow to cool, then sprinkle with confectioners' sugar.
Serve the apple strudel warm (with warm vanilla sauce) or cold, garnish with cream, as desired.

Topfen Strudel

INGREDIENTS

Strudel pastry, ready-made or self-made

FILLING

500 g (18 oz.) softened quark (farmer's cheese) 20 % fat
60 g (2.1 oz.) raisins soaked in rum
100 g (3.5 oz.) sour cream
100 g (3.5 oz.) butter, room temperature
60 g (2.1 oz.) superfine (caster) sugar
60 g (2.1 oz.) confectioners' sugar
6 egg yolks, 6 egg whites
Juice from 1 lemon
Grated zest from 1/2 organic lemon
1 tbsp vanilla custard powder
Pulp from 1 vanilla bean
Pinch of salt
1 egg for daubing
Butter for daubing

❶ Use the recipe on p. 46 to prepare the strudel pastry. Place it on top of a tea towel dusted with flour and roll it out.

❷ For the filling, cut the butter into pieces and put into a mixing bowl. Add the confectioners' sugar, vanilla pulp, grated lemon zest and salt. Mix everything with an egg whisk until smooth and creamy. Gradually stir the egg yolk and custard powder into the butter. Then, mix the mass with the quark, sour cream, rum-raisins and lemon juice. Beat the egg white with the superfine sugar until fluffy and fold in.

❸ Then, continue as with the apple strudel recipe (see above) until the sprinkling of the crumbs (in step 3). The process is as follows: daub the strudel pastry with butter, place the quark filling on top, and roll the strudel pastry.

❹ Lift the strudel onto a deep baking tray greased with butter; daub with a beaten egg and bake in a preheated for approx. 20 minutes at 170°C (340°F). Then reduce the temperature to 120°C (250°F), and finish baking the strudel for approx. another 10 minutes. While the strudel is baking, intermittently brush it with butter.

❺ Allow the strudel to cool a little, then sprinkle with confectioners' sugar.

Sacher Cubes

Yields 24 pieces

INGREDIENTS

1 Sacher-Torte cake
  mixture
300 g (10.5 oz.) puréed
  apricot jam
Shortening for greasing
Flour for dusting

FROSTING

180 g (2.8 oz.) chocolate
200 g (1 cup) superfine
  (caster) sugar
2 tbsp apricot jam
1/4 l (1 cup) water

❶ Prepare the Sacher-Torte cake mixture from p. 119. Grease 2 trays with butter and dust with flour (throw off the excess flour). Then spread the cake mixture about 2cm (approx. 1 inch) high over the tray. Bake in a preheated, fan-assisted oven at 220°C (425°F) for approx. 15 minutes. Remove from the oven and allow to cool. In the meantime, warm up the apricot jam, stirring until smooth. Spread a thick layer of apricot jam over the chocolate sponge base. Fold the sponge base with the jam side over on top of itself and immediately put it in the freezer (or in the fridge) and freeze because they dry easily.

❷ Now, for the frosting, break the chocolate into pieces and melt in a bain-marie. Boil the water and sugar, letting it boil for five minutes, bubbling. Then, while stirring, pour in the melted chocolate; stir in a tablespoon of apricot jam. Use a hand-held mixer to mix the chocolate mass until it has cooled down to 38°C/100°F (push the hand blender deep enough so that there are no air bubbles on the surface – the confectioners' terminology for this is "a perfect emulsion without an air pocket.")

❸ Next, take the chocolate sponge out of the freezer or fridge and cut it into 24 nice, equally sized cubes of 3x3 cm (1x1 inch). Heat up the left over apricot jam; put the Sacher cubes on a cake rack and cover with the hot jam. Smooth over the jam using a spatula and let "draw" for a few minutes. Finally, put the frosting on the Sacher cubes and smooth it over with the spatula.

Swiss Roll

INGREDIENTS

5 egg whites, cooled
4 egg yolks
250 g (1/2 pound) apricot jam
70 g (2.5 oz.) superfine (caster) sugar
1 tsp vanilla sugar
40 g (1.4 oz.) fine flour
40 g (1.4 oz.) cornstarch
20 g (4 tsp) melted butter
4 cl (8 tsp) apricot brandy
1 pinch salt
Confectioners' sugar for dusting

❶ Put the flour and cornstarch through a sieve. Place the cold egg white and the superfine sugar and vanilla sugar as well as the salt also in a cold bowl and, using a hand mixer (middle setting), beat until stiff – the egg white should have a creamy consistency. Gradually fold the egg yolks into the whites, and stir in the melted butter. Fold the flour/cornstarch mixture carefully into the egg-white/yolk mass.

❷ Put baking paper on a tray and spread over about a finger width of the sponge mixture. Smooth it as much as possible and bake in a preheated oven at 220°C (425°F) for about 8–10 minutes until the surface of the sponge begins to dry. Remove from the oven and turn upside down onto a sufficiently sized piece of baking paper or a tea towel sprinkled with confectioners' sugar.

❸ Carefully peel off the baking paper (from what is now the top of the sponge). If it sticks, brush with some cold water. Immediately warm up the apricot jam, stir in the apricot brandy and spread onto the sponge surface. Carefully roll up the cake and wrap it in baking paper, and leave it to cool. Remove the paper and dust with confectioners' sugar.

TIP: A Swiss roll is perfect for freezing and for this reason can be reserved for surprise guests. And you can also prepare it with other jams, according to taste. Or with a non-puréed jam that has whole fruit pieces.

Cream Slices

Yields about 12 slices

INGREDIENTS

400 g (14 oz.) pastry, home- or ready-made
1/2 l (2 cups) heavy cream
80 g (2.8 oz.) superfine (caster) sugar
1 tbsp vanilla sugar
3 eggs
5 egg yolks
4 cl (8 tsp) rum
Pulp from 1 vanilla bean
6 sheets gelatin
1 pinch salt
Apricot jam for brushing
Fondant for the frosting

❶ Soak the gelatin in cold water. Then, firstly, over a warm bain-marie, then a cold one, beat the eggs, egg yolks, both sugars, vanilla pulp, rum and salt until fluffy. Drain the gelatin and heat it up in a little water. Then fold the gelatin into the egg-sugar mixture. Whip the cream until stiff and carefully fold into the mass. Fill a square baking tray, approx. 30x20 cm (12x8 inches), with the vanilla-cream mixture and refrigerate.

❷ Thinly roll out the pastry (home- or ready-made) on a floured surface and cut out two 30x20 cm (12x8 inches) squares. Place them on a baking tray lined with baking paper, and pierce each pastry several times with a fork and let sit for 20 minutes. Afterward, bake in a preheated oven at 180°C (350°F) for 15–20 minutes. Leave to cool down.

❸ Then, warm up the apricot jam. Turn over the pastry squares and, on the smooth side, brush with the jam. Warm up the fondant (to approx. 40°C/100°F). Glaze one of the pastry squares thinly with fondant and dry in an oven at 60°C (140°F). Take the tray of well cooled cream out of the fridge and, directly from the tray, turn the cream upside down (as precisely as possible) over the unglazed piece of pastry. Cover with the cooled, glazed piece of pastry, and cut into slices.

Kardinalschnitten

(Cardinal Slices)

Yields 8 slices

INGREDIENTS

FOR MIXTURE I
(EGG WHITES)

9 egg whites
240 g (8.5 oz.) confectioners'
sugar
1 tsp vanilla sugar
1 pinch salt
Confectioners' sugar for
dusting

FOR MIXTURE II
(YOLK MASS)

3 eggs
4 egg yolks
80 g (2.8 oz.) confectioners'
sugar
75 g (2.6 oz.) fine flour
Zest from an untreated lemon

FOR MIXTURE II
(CREAM)

300 g (10.5 oz.) fresh
raspberries
3 cl (6 tsp) raspberry brandy
400 ml (13.5 fl. oz.) heavy
cream
40 g (1.4 oz.) confectioners'
sugar
2 tbsp instant coffee powder
2 sheets gelatin, soaked in
water
2 cl (4 tsp) egg liquor
1 pinch salt
1 handful slivered almonds,
roasted
Confectioners' sugar for
dusting

❶ Firstly, cut out two strips of baking paper (14x35 cm/5.5x14 inches), and place on a baking tray. Then, for mixture I, beat the egg whites with the confectioners' sugar, vanilla sugar and salt until stiff. For mixture II, beat the eggs with the yolks, confectioners' sugar and grated lemon zestuntil fluffy and fold in the sieved flour, combining it well with the mass.

❷ Carefully fill the egg white mixture into in a pastry bag with a large, smooth spout and squeeze out onto the baking paper three long strips spaced about 2cm (approx. 1 inch) apart. Now, with mixture II – the egg-yolk mass – use a similar (or the same, cleaned) pastry bag, to squeeze out strips between the egg-white strips. On each piece of baking paper there should be 3 strips of egg white and, in between, 2 yolk-mass strips. Generously dust these with confectioners' sugar and, in a preheated oven at 180°C (350°F) with the door slightly open (use a cooking spoon to keep it open, if needed), bake dry (rather than bake) for about 20–25 minutes. Let the 2 layers cool and turn over onto a tray; carefully remove the baking paper (brush with cold water if it sticks).

❸ For mixture III, marinade the washed and patted dry raspberries in brandy. Whip the cream with the instant coffee until stiff. Soak and drain the gelatin. Heat up the Advocat and stir in the gelatin until it dissolves. Fold the egg-gelatin mass, confectioners' sugar and salt into the whipped cream. Refrigerate briefly and allow to thicken. Then, fill the cream mixture into a pastry bag and squeeze half of it onto the first layer of pastry. Distribute the marinated raspberries on top, and squeeze on the rest of the mixture. Finally, place the second layer of pastry carefully on top of the cream. Sprinkle with the slivered, roasted almonds. Dust with confectioners' sugar. Using a sharp knife, cut into 8 slices.

TIP: The cardinal slices can also be prepared using a lighter cream made from yoghurt (3.6 % fat) or farmer's cheese cream (40 %).

Kaiserschmarren
(Shredded Pancakes)

INGREDIENTS

250 ml (1 cup) milk
130 g (1 cup) fine flour
2 tbsp superfine (caster)
    sugar
1 tbsp vanilla sugar
6 tbsp raisins
6 egg yolks
6 egg whites
1 pinch salt
Lemon juice for seasoning
Butter
Confectioners' sugar for
    dusting

❶ Put the egg yolks in a bowl; add the milk, flour, vanilla sugar, rum, lemon juice, and salt and stir into a smooth batter using an egg whisk. In another bowl, beat the egg whites and sugar in a bowl until stiff.

❷ Carefully fold in the egg whites. In a large ovenproof pan on the stove, heat some butter, pour in the batter and in the hot butter, brown on both sides. Once both sides are done, put it into a preheated oven at 180°C (350°F) and bake until golden brown.

❸ Then remove the pan from the oven, and, using 2 forks, break the mass into pieces. Mix in the raisins and sprinkle with sugar. Put into the oven again briefly until the sugar is caramelized. Serve sprinkled with confectioners' sugar.
A classic side dish is plum sauce.

BY THE WAY: Did you know that the Kaisersemmel and the Kaiserschnitzel already existed in Vienna before Emperor Franz Joseph I reigned? As also with the Kaiserwetter, a cloudless, deep blue and sunny sky, the imperial term indicated that it was something to do with what an emperor (Kaiser) himself would like. Only Kaiserschmarren – and this is guaranteed – really made Franz Joseph happy. His modesty in things culinary made him likeable to many people: the highest and most powerful man hardly ate anything other than what the simple man ate.

Wachauer Apricot Dumplings

Yields 12 dumplings

INGREDIENTS

500 g (18 oz.) softened quark, 20 % fat
150 g (5.2 oz.) flour
150 g (5.2 oz.) fine hard wheat semolina
3 egg yolks
3 egg whites
120 g (4.2 oz.) butter
Pulp from 1 vanilla bean
1 pinch salt
Approx. 4cl (8 tsp) apricot brandy for the cooking water
Approx. 2 tbsp sugar for the cooking water
Confectioners' sugar for dusting

FILLING

12 small, ripe apricots
12 almonds, peeled and roasted
80 g (2.8 oz.) marzipan
1–2 dashes Amaretto

BUTTER CRUMBS

300 g (10.5 oz.) breadcrumbs
150 g (5.2 oz.) butter
60 g (2.1 oz.) superfine (caster) sugar
20 g (4 tsp) vanilla sugar
Cinnamon

❶ For the dumplings, whip the butter until fluffy. Add the egg yolk and stir. Then add the semolina, egg whites, vanilla pulp and a pinch of salt and fold in with an egg whisk. Then, in turn, add the flour and the quark, stirring until a smooth dough is formed. Make a roll out of the dough, wrap in plastic wrap, and leave to rise for about 1 hour.

❷ For the filling, wash and dry the apricots. Knead the marzipan with a bit of Amaretto. Then cut or break off small pieces of marzipan, flatten it and put an almond on each piece and wrap the almond in the marzipan. Press the stones out of the apricots without cutting them. Into the cavity of each, push in one almond wrapped in marzipan.

❸ After an hour, take the dough out of the refrigerator and cut into 12 equal slices. Flatten the slices from the middle and place an apricot in the center. Wrap the fruit in the dough and form smooth dumplings.

❹ Boil some water in a large pot with some sugar, the apricot brandy and a pinch of salt. Place the dumplings in boiling water, then turn down the heat and simmer for about 15 minutes until they rise to the surface.

❺ While the dumplings are cooking, heat some butter in a pan for the crumbs. Combine the crumbs, sugar, vanilla sugar, and cinnamon, if desired, and put in the pan. Over low heat, fry golden brown, stirring regularly.

❻ Remove the dumplings using a strainer ladle. Drain well and carefully toss them in the crumbs, then arrange on plates and serve using the rest of the butter crumbs from the pan and dust with confectioners' sugar.

TIP: These Wachau apricot dumplings are a somewhat "finer" version of the classic apricot dumplings made from potato dough, in which the apricot stone is simply replaced with a piece of cubed sugar.

Dukatenbuchteln
(Baked Yeast Buns with Vanilla Sauce)

INGREDIENTS
250 g (2 cups) fine flour
10 g (2 tsp) yeast
100 ml (3.4 fl. oz.) milk
35 g (1.2 oz.) sugar
40 g (1.4 oz.) soft butter
2 egg yolks
**Grated zest from
    1/2 untreated lemon**
Melted butter
**Flour for the work
    surface**
**Confectioners' sugar
    for dusting**

VANILLA SAUCE
150 ml (5 fl. oz.) milk
**125 ml (1/2 cup) cream,
    whipped semi-stiff**
1/2 vanilla bean
**60 g (2.1 oz.) superfine
    (caster) sugar**
3 egg yolks

❶ For the sponge – the preferment – warm up the milk and pour into a bowl. Crumble the yeast and stir into the lukewarm milk. Add approx. 1/3 of the flour and stir until smooth together with the milk and yeast. Now sprinkle the sponge mixture – which should be soft and smooth – lightly with flour, cover it and leave to rise in a warm place. Then, mix the rest of the flour, 2 egg yolks, sugar, pinch of salt and lemon zest well into the dough. Finally, work in the soft butter and knead and beat the dough (hard onto the work surface) until the dough separates itself from the bottom of the bowl in one piece. Then cover the bowl again and leave the dough to rise in a warm place until the volume has increased considerably in size.

❷ On a floured surface, roll the dough flat to about 2 cm (less than an inch). With a cutter (or an upside down glass), cut out pieces about 6 cm (2 inches) in diameter. The dough pieces are made into "buchteln" by folding the edges of each piece upwards and closing the edges tightly at the top.

❸ Now, preheat the oven, grease the baking tray. Melt enough butter in a pot on the stove. One by one, dip each piece in the melted butter and place them closely side-by-side in a well-greased baking tray with the folded edge facing down. Bake in a preheated oven at 180°C (350°F) for about 20–30 minutes until golden brown. Before serving, dust with confectioners' sugar.

❹ For the vanilla sauce, cut the half vanilla bean lengthwise without scraping out the pulp. Heat up the milk, add the vanilla bean, and steep for 5 minutes over low heat, then remove from the milk. In a bowl, beat the egg yolks and sugar. Fold the egg-sugar mass into the cooled milk and, over low heat, keep stirring until the sauce thickens slightly. Place the pot in a bowl filled with ice water and allow to cool, stirring now and again. When the sauce is cold, fold in some whipped cream.

❺ Before serving, pour some vanilla sauce on a plate and place the buns on top.

TIP: The origin for the names "buchteln" or "wuchtel" comes from the Czech verb "to swell" – as a yeast dough, during preparation, it increases considerably in size. The additional "dukaten" in Viennese traditionally stands for particularly "fine" ones, that is, buchteln that are so golden in appearance that they look like ducats. By the way, you can fill them by putting plum or apricot jam inside the raw dough before folding in the sides.

Sacher

Powidltascherln
(Plum Jam Turnovers)

INGREDIENTS

150 g (5.2 oz.) plum jam
150 g (5.2 oz.) fine flour
300 ml (1.2 cups) milk
2 egg yolks
2 tbsp butter
2 cl (4 tsp) rum or plum schnapps
1 pinch salt
1 egg for brushing
Confectioners' sugar for dusting

BUTTER CRUMBS

100 g (3.5 oz.) butter
100 g (3.5 oz.) breadcrumbs
50 g (1.7 oz.) ground walnuts
2 tbsp superfine (caster) sugar
1 tbsp vanilla sugar
1 pinch cinnamon, ground

❶ In a pot, boil the milk with the butter and a pinch of salt. Reduce the heat and gradually stir in the flour and keep stirring. Continue to stir until a very smooth dough is formed that easily separates from the bottom of the pot. Transfer it into a mixing bowl and quickly mix in the 2 egg yolks and allow to cool.

❷ Then, place the dough on a floured bread board. Dust the dough with flour and roll it out to about 4 mm (0.2 inch) thick. With a round cutter, cut 12 shapes (about 8 cm/3 inches in diameter). Mix the plum jam with the rum. Beat the eggs and brush the edges of the dough pieces with the egg. Spoon small portions of the rum/plum-jam mixture, a little off-center of the dough cuts. Fold over from the sides without jam and firmly press the edges together so that a half-moon shape is formed.

❸ Boil some salted water in a large pot; reduce the heat and place the plum pockets in the water. Simmer over low heat for about 5 minutes. (When the pockets rise to the surface they are done.)

❹ Meanwhile, melt the butter for the butter crumbs in a pan and fry the crumbs, nuts, sugar and vanilla and sugar and a pinch of cinnamon. Stir well and fry until golden brown.

❺ When the plum turnovers are ready, remove them from the pot with a strainer ladle and let drain. Then add them to the pan with the butter crumbs and toss until they are covered. Before serving, dust lightly with confectioners' sugar.

Sweet Sacher Recipes · Warm Desserts

Poppy Seed Noodles
with Plum Sauce

Yields approx. 6 portions

INGREDIENTS

DOUGH
500 g (18 oz.) floury potatoes
100 g (3.5 oz.) flour
50 g (1.7 oz.) hard wheat
    semolina
50 g (1.7 oz.) cornstarch
    (Maizena)
100 g (3.5 oz.) quark (20 % fat)
1 egg
1 egg yolk
40 g (1.4 oz.) butter
Nutmeg, freshly grated
Salt

POPPY SEED CRUMBS
150 g (5.2 oz.) poppy seeds,
    finely ground
4 tbsp confectioners' sugar
2 tbsp breadcrumbs
80 g (2.8 oz.) butter
4 cl (8 tsp) rum
Confectioners' sugar for
    dusting

PLUM SAUCE
500 g (18 oz.) small plums,
    not too soft
100 g (3.5 oz.) sugar
Zest from 1/2 untreated
    orange
Juice from 1 lemon
100 ml (3.4 fl. oz.) red wine
1 pinch cinnamon

❶ If you like, you can prepare the plum sauce beforehand. Wash and halve the plums, remove the stones. Heat up the sugar in a pot and caramelize it, stirring continuously. Pour in the red wine and reduce to half. Cut the orange peel in strips. Combine the plums, cinnamon, orange peel, and the red wine mixture, and simmer for approx. 8–10 minutes. Then remove the orange peel; season with some lemon juice and refrigerate. (Twenty minutes before serving, remove from the fridge so the aroma can develop.)

❷ For the dough, peel the potatoes and boil in lightly salted water. Let them cool a little, and then put through a potato ricer while still warm. On a work surface, combine the potatoes with the other ingredients: butter, egg, egg yolk, quark, semolina, cornstarch, the salt, and grated nutmeg, and work into a smooth, elastic dough. Form a thick roll, and using a cutter, cut out pieces about a thumb thickness wide. On a floured surface, roll small noodles out of the dough with a flat hand, or, as the say in Austria "wuzeln."

❸ In a large pot, boil some salted water and put the noodles in; reduce the heat and simmer, lightly bubbling, for about 5 minutes. Remove with a straining ladle (or drain the whole pot) and let drain.

❹ For the poppy seed crumbs, froth up the butter. Add the poppy seed crumbs, confectioners' sugar, and rum, and mix well. Toss the noodles well in the mixture. Serve dusted with confectioners' sugar and the plum sauce on the side.

Salzburger Nockerln
(Fluffy Egg Soufflé)

INGREDIENTS
150 ml (5 fl. oz.) milk
7 egg whites, cooled
4 egg yolks
80 g (2.8 oz.) superfine (caster) sugar
2 tbsp flour
1 tbsp cornstarch (Maizena)
1/2 vanilla bean
10 g (2 tsp) vanilla sugar
Zest from 1 lemon, grated
1 squeeze lemon juice
Butter for greasing
Confectioners' sugar for dusting

❶ Grease a heat-proof form – most suitably, an oval ovenproof dish – with butter. Heat the milk in a pot. Cut open the vanilla bean (without scraping out the pulp) and put it in the milk with a squeeze of lemon juice. Let boil once and immediately remove from the stove. Let sit for 5 minutes. Then remove the vanilla bean and pour enough vanilla milk into the dish so that it just covers the bottom.

❷ With a hand mixer, mix the 7 cooled egg whites with about 1/3 of the sugar, and a pinch of salt until very stiff. Slowly add the rest of the sugar and continue to beat until the mixture is not only thick but also creamy. Then add the 4 egg yolks, flour and cornstarch, vanilla sugar, as well as the grated lemon zest to the egg whites, and, using an egg whisk, fold three or four times (the mass shouldn't become homogenous). Then, make 4 pyramid shapes, placing them next to each other in the ovenproof dish. In a preheated oven at 220°C (425°F) bake for 10–12 minutes until golden brown. Remove from the oven, dust with confectioners' sugar, and serve immediately.

Baked Apple Wheels

Yields 6 portions:

INGREDIENTS

1/2 kg (1.1 pound) apples
(Jonagold, Golden Delicious)
25 g (5 tsp) confectioners'
sugar
Juice from 1 lemon
2 cl (4 tsp) rum
1 tbsp vanilla sugar
Cinnamon, ground
Oil
50 g (1.7 oz.) confectioners'
sugar for dusting

MILK DOUGH

150 ml (5 fl. oz.) milk
100 g (3.5 oz.) flour
2 egg yolks
2 egg whites
25 g (5 tsp) superfine
(caster) sugar
1 cooking spoon vanilla
sugar
30 ml (2 tbsp) oil
1 pinch salt

❶ First, squeeze the lemon, and mix the lemon juice in a small bowl with the rum and confectioners' sugar. Then peel the apples; de-core and cut the apples in slices ("wheels") of about 1cm (1/2 inch) thick. Quickly spread the lemon-juice-rum mixture over the apples and let stand on a cake rack for approx. 10 minutes.

❷ For the dough, in a bowl, combine 100 ml (3.4 fl. oz.) milk with the 2 egg yolks, oil, vanilla sugar, and salt. Sieve the flour, add it, and stir until smooth. Then fold in the rest of the 50 ml (1.7 fl. oz.) milk. In a second bowl, beat the 2 egg whites with the superfine (caster) sugar. Then carefully fold the whites into the dough mixture.

❸ Heat up some oil in a frying pan. Coat the apple pieces in the batter (they should be well covered all around) and fry on both sides in the hot oil until golden brown. When they are ready, remove them from the pan and let drain on kitchen paper. Mix a tablespoon of vanilla sugar with 50 g (1.7 oz.) confectioners' sugar and some ground cinnamon and sprinkle the apples with it.

TIP: The milk batter also goes well with other fruit, such as plums, apricots, peaches, etc.

Vanilla Kipferl

INGREDIENTS

50 g (1.7 oz.) almond semolina
50 g (1.7 oz.) hazelnut semolina
Pulp from 1 vanilla bean
70 g (2.5 oz.) confectioners' sugar
280 g (9.8 oz.) fine flour
200 g (7 oz.) butter, room temperature
2 egg yolks
1 pinch salt
Approx. 100 g (3.5 oz.) confectioners' sugar, mixed with some vanilla pulp, for dusting

● Knead the entire ingredients – flour, butter, confectioners' sugar, ground almonds and hazelnuts, yolks, vanilla pulp and pinch of salt – into a dough. Form small crescent shapes from the dough and place these on a tray lined with baking paper. Cover with aluminum foil and refrigerate overnight.
Then, in a preheated oven at 180°C (350°F), bake for about 8–10 minutes. Combine 100 g (3.5 oz.) confectioners' sugar with some vanilla pulp and sprinkle over the still warm kipferl.

Butter Florentines

INGREDIENTS

230 g (8 oz.) almonds, ground
70 g (2.5 oz.) honey
100 g (3.5 oz.) superfine (caster) sugar
30 ml (1 oz.) glucose (from a chemist)
50 ml (1.8 oz.) cream, 50 g (1.7 oz.) butter
50 g (1.7 oz.) candied orange peel, diced
30 g (6 tsp) candied cherries, chopped
230 g (8 oz.) milk chocolate (for dipping)
Butter for greasing
Flour for dusting

❶ Heat up the cream and butter, sugar, glucose and honey, reduce the heat and simmer. Stir in the ground almonds, orange peel and the chopped, candied cherries and lightly brown while stirring.

❷ Grease a baking tray with butter, and dust with flour. Using a small spoon, take some of the almond mixture, place it on the baking tray, and, using your hand – well moistened – to flatten the mass. When the almond dough has been used up and the tray is full of Florentines, put into a preheated oven (180°C/350°F), and first bake for 4 minutes. Then, if desired, use a round cutter to form more cookies. Let the cookies cool, and then, again at 180°C (350°F) – bake for 5 minutes (now they should look nicely golden brown and honey-glazed).

Elderberry Parfait
with rhubarb and fried blossoms

INGREDIENTS

PARFAIT

190 ml (6.4 oz.) elderberry syrup
500 ml (17 oz.) cream, whipped
6 egg whites
120 g (4.2 oz.) sugar
4 sheets gelatin, soaked and drained
Juice from 1 lime
Baking tray with aluminum foil

RHUBARB SAUCE

400 g (2 cups) rhubarb, finely cut
100 g (3.5 oz.) sugar
Lemon juice, as desired

BAKED ELDERBERRIES

4 nice elderberry blossoms
120 ml (4 fl. oz.) milk
2 egg yolks
2 egg whites
90 g (3.2 oz.) flour
3 tbsp oil
15 g (0.5 oz.) sugar
1 pinch salt
Oil

❶ For the parfait, beat the 6 egg whites with the sugar over a bain-marie at approx. 40°C (100°F) until fluffy. Warm up some elderberry syrup and dissolve the well-drained gelatin in it. Then pour in the rest of the syrup and lime juice; stir well. Now, carefully combine the egg whites and the syrup, and fold in the whipped cream. Spread the mass on a baking tray lined with aluminum foil, and freeze.

❷ For the rhubarb sauce, peel the rhubarb, cut it into small pieces, and put in a bowl. Add sugar, mix it with the rhubarb, and allow to draw for 2 hours. Then, put into an oven-proof dish and, in a preheated oven, bake at 180°C (350°F) for about 10 minutes. When the rhubarb is al dente, drain it. Season the liquid with some lemon juice and thicken with the Maizena. Add the drained rhubarb pieces to the liquid again.

❸ For the dough, beat the 2 egg yolks in a bowl; add milk and oil, and stir until smooth. Sieve the flour and fold it in. Whisk the egg white until stiff, and gradually sprinkle in the sugar and a pinch of salt. Slowly fold the egg whites into the dough mass. Stir the elderberry blossoms through the batter and, with the stem pointing upwards, fry in a pan with hot oil until golden brown.

❹ Then, take the baking tray out of the freezer and turn it over. Cut the parfait into medium-sized squares and place one each in the middle of a plate. Place some rhubarb sauce next to it. Decoratively arrange the elderberry blossoms, and sprinkle with confectioners' sugar.

Basic Recipe for Sorbet

Yields 4–5 portions

INGREDIENTS

375 g (1.5 cups) fruit pulp, as desired (e.g. peach, blueberry, strawberry, mango, etc.)

75 g (2.6 oz.) superfine (caster) sugar

75 g (2.6 oz.) glucose (from the chemist)

Approx. 180 ml (6 fl. oz.) water

Lemon juice

● Put some water in a pot; stir in the sugar and glucose (sugar syrup) and bring to the boil. Add the fruit pulp and stir well, possibly season with some lemon juice. Let cool, and then, either freeze in an ice-maker or use a freezing container, and place in the freezer for about 4 hours. Here, it's important that you stir it around roughly every 30 minutes (with an egg whisk or fork) to disperse the ice crystals that form during the freezing process, and to make sure that the sorbet takes on a creamy consistency.

TIP: Don't serve the sorbet directly from the freezer, but allow it to defrost beforehand.

Crêpe Slices
with lemon mousse and melissa sorbet

For a spring form of 26 cm (10 inches) Ø

INGREDIENTS

CRÊPES
500 ml (2.1 cups) milk
200 g (7 oz.) flour
4 eggs
Pulp from 1 vanilla bean
Salt
Some shortening or oil

LEMON-CHOCOLATE MOUSSE
100 ml (3.4 fl. oz.) lemon juice
Grated untreated lemon zest
350 g (12.3 oz.) white chocolate
300 ml (1.2 cups) heavy cream
90 ml (3 fl. oz.) milk
6 sheets gelatin, soaked in water and drained

MELISSA SORBET
200 g (1 cup) superfine (caster) sugar
1 grated lemon zest
Juice from 4 lemons
30 g (2 tbsp) melissa, finely cut
100 ml (3.4 fl. oz.) white wine
2 egg whites
2 tbsp sugar

❶ For the melissa sorbet, add the sugar and lemon zest to about 440 ml (2 cups) water and bring to the boil. Let cool and then pour in the lemon juice and white wine. Add the finely chopped melissa and mix with a hand blender. Let rest for 2 hours, then, either freeze it in an ice-maker, or use a freezing container, and place it in the freezer, stirring it around with an egg whisk or fork regularly. Shortly before serving, beat the 2 egg whites with 2 tablespoons of sugar until fluffy, fold it in so that the sorbet becomes light and creamy.

❷ While the sorbet is freezing, beat the eggs with the milk, some salt and vanilla pulp; add flour and stir until smooth. In a crêpe or pancake pan, heat up some oil or shortening. Pour in some batter, smooth it over and fry one side golden brown and then the other. Let it glide off the pan onto a plate and continue making the thin crêpes. If necessary, cut to the diameter of the cake form (26 cm/10 inches Ø).

❸ For the mousse, boil the milk with the grated lemon zest; let it simmer, and then pass through a fine sieve. Melt the white chocolate; add to the milk and mix both well with a hand blender. Warm up the lemon juice, dissolve the gelatin in it, and then mix the juice and the chocolate mass together with a hand blender. Allow to cool. Whip the cream, and carefully fold it into the mass.

❹ Place some aluminum foil on a baking tray. Put the cake ring on top and fill it with the crêpes and the mousse, alternately. Begin with a crêpe, then spread about 80 g (2.8 oz.) mousse over evenly, add the next crêpe, and continue the process. Keep repeating until the desired height of the crêpe slices is reached (ideally, 6–8 layers). Finish with a crêpe. Put the remaining cream in a pastry bag with a smooth spout and decorate the cake with daubs of cream. Refrigerate.

❺ Before serving, remove the cake ring, and cut the crêpe cake. Serve one crêpe per plate and place the melissa sorbet dumpling next to it. Garnish with fresh mint.

TIP: Serve with berries marinated in confectioners' sugar and lemon juice.

Semolina Flammerie
with fruit minestrone

INGREDIENTS

FLAMMERIE

40 g (1.4 oz.) semolina
250 ml (1 cup) milk
190 ml (6.4 fl. oz.) cream
2 egg yolks
65 g (2.3 oz.) confectioners'
    sugar
Zest from 1/2 lemon
Zest from 1/2 orange
Pulp from 1 vanilla bean
3 sheets gelatin, soaked in
    water

FRUIT MINESTRONE

500 g (18 oz.) seasonal
    fruit (strawberries, kiwi,
    pineapple, mango, pink
    grapefruit, berries,
    melons, etc.)
1 l (4.2 cups) water
360 g (12.7 oz.) sugar
30 ml (6 tsp) lime juice
1/2 vanilla bean
1 stalk lemon grass
1 sprig basil
1 sprig mint
1 sprig lemon thyme
1 sprig verbena
1/2 star anise
3 g (1/2 tsp) Xanthan

❶ Boil the milk with the vanilla pulp, the grated lemon and orange zest, and then strain it through a sieve. Bring to the boil again and stir in the semolina. Now bring the semolina to the boil and stir in the gelatin. Allow to cool. Beat the egg yolk and confectioners' sugar until fluffy, and stir into the cooled semolina. Whip the cream and fold it in. Make some forms out of foil and fill them with the semolina mass. Refrigerate.

❷ For the fruit minestrone, first boil the sugar and water into a syrup. Then add the lime juice, spices and herbs (vanilla, lemon grass, basil, mint, lemon thyme, verbena, star anise; keep a few mint leaves for the garnish). Let sit for about 1 hour. Strain through a sieve and mix with the Xanthana. Refrigerate.

❸ Wash and dry the fruit. Then, where possible, cube or cut. Arrange the fruit pieces on deep plates and pour on some aromatic syrup. Place the semolina flammerie on top. Garnish with mint leaves.

Semolina Dumplings

with wild berries and mint granité

INGREDIENTS

DUMPLINGS

170 g (5.9 oz.) semolina
1/2 l (2.1 cups) milk
120 g (4.2 oz.) soft butter
3 tbsp sugar
3 eggs
1 vanilla bean
Zest from 1/2 lemon, grated
Zest from 1 orange, grated
10 g (2 tsp) sugar
10 g (2 tsp) salt
1 pinch salt
Breadcrumbs
Some sugar

WILD BERRY SAUCE

500 g (18 oz.) mixed wild
  berries
200 g (7 oz.) preserving sugar
  (1:1)
20 g (4 tsp) raspberry brandy

MINT GRANITÉ

250 ml (1 cup) water
50 ml (1.7 fl. oz.) lemon juice
100 g (3.5 oz.) sugar
50 g (1.7 oz.) fresh mint

❶ Combine the milk, vanilla bean and the grated lemon zest. Stir in the butter, pinch of salt and sugar, then fold in the semolina. Before the mass begins to harden, beat the eggs and quickly stir them in. Mix well, then refrigerate the semolina mass for 2 hours.

❷ Fill a pot with about 1 liter (4.2 cups) water; add 10 g (2 tsp) sugar, 10 g (2 tsp) salt and the grated orange zest. Heat up the water. Form dumplings from the semolina mass with moist hands. Bring the water to the boil, reduce the heat. Put the dumplings in and let simmer for approx. 15 minutes. Fry some breadcrumbs in a frying pan (possibly add some butter), mix with the sugar and coat the semolina dumplings in it.

❸ For the wild berry sauce, cook the washed and cleaned berries in the preserving sugar for about 5 minutes, then stir in the raspberry brandy. Allow to cool.

❹ For the granité, boil some water with the lemon juice, sugar and the mint. Allow to cool a little and then put in a bowl and freeze. Later, scrape out the frozen granité with a fork.

❺ Before serving, place the lukewarm wild berry sauce in the middle of some plates and position 2 dumplings per plate on top. Serve the granité separately in small bowls.

A NOTE ABOUT MEASUREMENTS

Measurements of dry ingredients in American, British and Australian recipes are usually listed by volume. European recipes on the other hand, are measured by weight. Below is a conversion table for your convenience.

The cups, ounces and tablespoon measurements given in parentheses throughout this book refer to US standard measurements.

The following conversions may be useful:

1 teaspoon	1/3 tablespoon	1/6 ounce		5 ml
1 tablespoon	3 teaspoons	1/2 ounce		14 grams
16 tablespoons	1 cup	8 ounces	0.500 pound or 1/2 pound	225 grams

1 g = 0.035 ounces   1 ounce = 28.349 g   100 g = 3.5 ounces/0.423 cup
1 US cup = 237 millilitres (ml)   1 UK, Australian or Canadian cup = 250 ml
1 standard US tablespoon (tbsp) = 15 ml   1 standard UK tbsp = 15 ml
1 standard Australian tbsp = 20 ml   1 standard Canadian tbsp = 15 ml

Teaspoons (tsp) can be converted 1:1

For the best results, we recommend weighing the ingredients with kitchen scales. All recipes yield 4 servings, if not otherwise specified.

Recipe Index

Sacher

IMPRINT

ISBN 978-3-85431-662-6

sty̆ria

© 2014 by Pichler Verlag in
Verlagsgruppe Styria GmbH & Co KG
Vienna · Graz · Klagenfurt

Books from Verlagsgruppe Styria
are available for purchase in all
book stores and online.

styriabooks.at

*Sacher chef Werner Pichlmaier (center) with his
cookbook team: Barbara Brunner, Franziska
Ettmeier, Manuel Weißenböck and Luisa Martini
(from left to right)*

Photos of the dishes:
Michael Rathmayer
Photos of the vignettes: iStockphoto.com
Recipes: Werner Pichlmaier
Editing: Birgit Schwaner
Editing assistance:
Gerd Wolfgang Sievers
Translation: Mỹ Huê McGowran

Project management:
Johannes Sachslehner
Cover and book design:
Bruno Wegscheider

Reproduction: Pixelstorm, Wien
Printing and binding:
Druckerei Theiss GmbH
St. Stefan im Lavanttal

7 6 5 4 3 2 1
Printed in Austria

*The editorial team and the publisher would like to
thank Hans Peter Fink, chef at Hotel Sacher Vienna
until 2008, for permission to use the recipes created
by him.*

*Last but not least, a very big thank you also to our
Managing Director Reiner Heilmann and to the
Assistant to the Manager Director Claudia Pichlmaier,
who both played a decisive role in the realization of
this book.*

*One of the traditional companies with whom Hotel
Sacher works is the glass manufacturing company
LOBMEYR, founded in 1823, which, in 1835, on
the occasion of the delivery of first services to the
imperial house, rose to become the Imperial & Royal
court supplier. J. & L. Lobmeyr generously supplied
glasses for the photo work, thus substantially
contributing to the success of this book. The editor
and publisher extend a hearty thanks to them for
their support.*